Pearson Edexcel GCSE (9-1)

History

Superpower relations and the Cold War, 1941–91

Series Editor: Angela Leonard   Authors: Christopher Catherwood   Nigel Kelly   Ben Armstrong

Published by Pearson Education Limited, 80 Strand, London, WC2R 0RL.

www.pearsonschoolsandfecolleges.co.uk

Copies of official specifications for all Edexcel qualifications may be found on the website: www.edexcel.com

Text © Pearson Education Limited 2018

Series editor: Angela Leonard
Designed by Colin Tilley Loughrey, Pearson Education Limited
Typeset by QBS Learning
Original illustrations © Pearson Education Limited
Illustrated by KJA Artists Illustration Agency, Phoenix Photosetting, Chatham, Kent and QBS Learning.

Cover design by Colin Tilley Loughrey
Cover photo © Getty Images: adoc-photos/Corbis

The rights of Christopher Catherwood, Nigel Kelly and Ben Armstrong to be identified as author of this work have been asserted by them in accordance with the Copyright, Designs and Patents Act 1988.

First published 2018

21 20 19 18
10 9 8 7 6 5 4 3 2 1

British Library Cataloguing in Publication Data
A catalogue record for this book is available from the British Library.
ISBN 978 1 292 25831 7

Printed in the UK by Bell and Bain Ltd, Glasgow

A note from the publisher
1. While the publishers have made every attempt to ensure that advice on the qualifications and its assessment is accurate, the official specification and associated guidance materials are the only authoritative source of information and should always be referred to for definitive guidance. Pearson examiners have not contributed to any sections in this resource relevant to examination papers for which they have responsibility.
2. Pearson has robust editorial processes, including answer and fact checks, to ensure the accuracy of the content in this publication, and every effort is made to ensure this publication is free of errors. We are, however, only human, and occasionally errors do occur. Pearson is not liable for any misunderstandings that arise as a result of errors in this publication, but it is our priority to ensure that the content is accurate. If you spot an error, please do contact us at resourcescorrections@pearson.com so we can make sure it is corrected.

Websites
Pearson Education Limited is not responsible for the content of any external internet sites. It is essential for tutors to preview each website before using it in class so as to ensure that the URL is still accurate, relevant and appropriate. We suggest that tutors bookmark useful websites and consider enabling students to access them through the school/college intranet.

Contents

How to use this book

What's covered?

This book covers the Period Study on Superpower Relations and the Cold War, 1941–91. This unit makes up 20% of your GCSE course, and will be examined in Paper 2.

Period studies cover a specific period of time of around 50 years, and require you to know about and be able to analyse the events surrounding important developments and issues that happened in this period. You need to understand how the different topics covered fit into the overall narrative. This book also explains the different types of exam questions you will need to answer, and includes advice and example answers to help you improve.

Features

As well as a clear, detailed explanation of the key knowledge you will need, you will also find a number of features in the book:

Key terms

Where you see a word followed by an asterisk, like this: Hawks and Doves*, you will be able to find a Key Terms box on that page that explains what the word means.

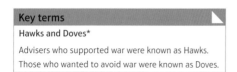

Key terms

Hawks and Doves*

Advisers who supported war were known as Hawks. Those who wanted to avoid war were known as Doves.

Activities

Every few pages, you'll find a box containing some activities designed to help check and embed knowledge and get you to really think about what you've studied. The activities start simple, but might get more challenging as you work through them.

Summaries and Checkpoints

At the end of each chunk of learning, the main points are summarised in a series of bullet points – great for embedding the core knowledge, and handy for revision.

Checkpoints help you to check and reflect on your learning. The Strengthen section helps you to consolidate knowledge and understanding, and check that you've grasped the basic ideas and skills.

The Challenge questions push you to go beyond just understanding the information, and into evaluation and analysis of what you've studied.

Sources and Interpretations

Although source work and interpretations do not appear in Paper 2, you'll still find interesting contemporary material throughout the books, showing what people from the period said, thought or created, helping you to build your understanding of people in the past.

Source E

A photograph of children watching as a supply plane arrives in Berlin during the Berlin Airlift.

Interpretation 1

A recent account of the Paris Summit meeting and U-2 incident from the *US Department of State Official History* website.

Khrushchev had publicly committed himself to the idea of 'peaceful coexistence*' with the United States... [Had] the United States apologized, he would have continued the summit. Eisenhower, however, refused to issue a formal apology... On May 11, Eisenhower finally acknowledged his full awareness of the entire program and of the Powers flight in particular. Moreover, he explained that... such spy flights were a necessary element in maintaining national defense, and that he planned to continue them.

Extend your knowledge

These features contain useful additional information that adds depth to your knowledge, and to your answers. The information is closely related to the key issues in the unit, and questions are sometimes included, helping you to link the new details to the main content.

Extend your knowledge

More about Marshall Aid

Marshall Aid was not just loans and grants of money to European governments. It also involved giving money to help groups in need. So it included nets for Norwegian fishermen, mules for Greek farmers and food for starving people.

Exam-style questions and tips

The book also includes extra exam-style questions you can use to practise. These appear in the chapters and are accompanied by a tip to help you get started on an answer.

Exam-style question, Section A
Explain **two** consequences of the Hungarian Uprising in 1956. **8 marks**

Exam tip
To avoid just describing, you could try using sentences that start like this: 'As a result of this event…', 'The effect of this was…', 'This led to…'

Recap pages

At the end of each chapter, you'll find a page designed to help you to consolidate and reflect on the chapter as a whole. Each recap page includes a recall quiz, ideal for quickly checking your knowledge or for revision. Recap pages also include activities designed to help you summarise and analyse what you've learned, and also reflect on how each chapter links to other parts of the unit.

THINKING HISTORICALLY

These activities are designed to help you develop a better understanding of how history is constructed, and are focused on the key areas of Evidence, Interpretations, Cause & Consequence and Change & Continuity. In the Period Study, you will come across an activity on Cause & Consequence, as this is a key focus for this unit.

The Thinking Historically approach has been developed in conjunction with Dr Arthur Chapman and the Institute of Education, UCL. It is based on research into the misconceptions that can hold students back in history.

THINKING HISTORICALLY ▶ Cause and Consequence (2c) ——— conceptual map reference

The Thinking Historically conceptual map can be found at: www.pearsonschools.co.uk/thinkinghistoricallygcse

WRITING HISTORICALLY

At the end of each chapter is a spread dedicated to helping you improve your writing skills. These include simple techniques you can use in your writing to make your answers clearer, more precise and better focused on the question you're answering.

The Writing Historically approach is based on the *Grammar for Writing* pedagogy developed by a team at the University of Exeter and popular in many English departments. Each spread uses examples from the preceding chapter, so it's relevant to what you've just been studying.

Preparing for your exams

At the back of the book, you'll find a special section dedicated to explaining and exemplifying the new Edexcel GCSE History exams. Advice on the demands of this paper, written by Angela Leonard, helps you prepare for and approach the exam with confidence. Each question type is explained through annotated sample answers at two levels, showing clearly how answers can be improved.

Pearson Progression Scale: This icon indicates the Step that a sample answer has been graded at on the Pearson Progression Scale.

This book is also available as an online ActiveBook, which can be licensed for your whole institution.

Timeline: Superpower relations and the Cold War, 1941–91

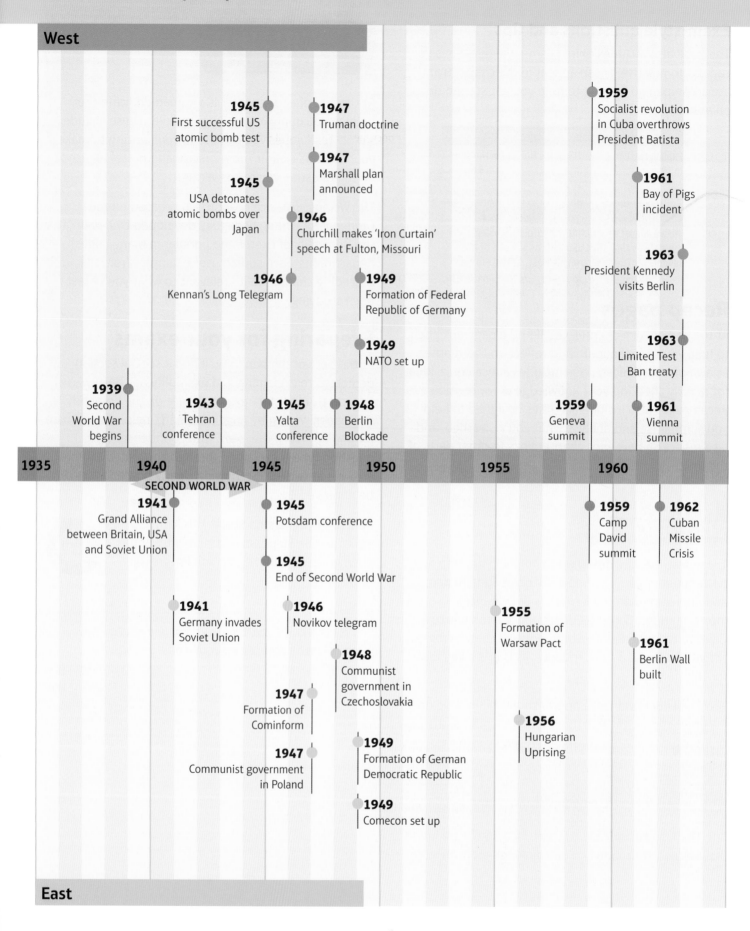

West

1945 First successful US atomic bomb test

1947 Truman doctrine

1959 Socialist revolution in Cuba overthrows President Batista

1947 Marshall plan announced

1945 USA detonates atomic bombs over Japan

1961 Bay of Pigs incident

1946 Churchill makes 'Iron Curtain' speech at Fulton, Missouri

1946 Kennan's Long Telegram

1949 Formation of Federal Republic of Germany

1963 President Kennedy visits Berlin

1949 NATO set up

1963 Limited Test Ban treaty

1939 Second World War begins

1943 Tehran conference

1945 Yalta conference

1948 Berlin Blockade

1959 Geneva summit

1961 Vienna summit

1935 | 1940 | 1945 | 1950 | 1955 | 1960

SECOND WORLD WAR

1941 Grand Alliance between Britain, USA and Soviet Union

1945 Potsdam conference

1959 Camp David summit

1962 Cuban Missile Crisis

1945 End of Second World War

1941 Germany invades Soviet Union

1946 Novikov telegram

1955 Formation of Warsaw Pact

1961 Berlin Wall built

1948 Communist government in Czechoslovakia

1947 Formation of Cominform

1956 Hungarian Uprising

1947 Communist government in Poland

1949 Formation of German Democratic Republic

1949 Comecon set up

East

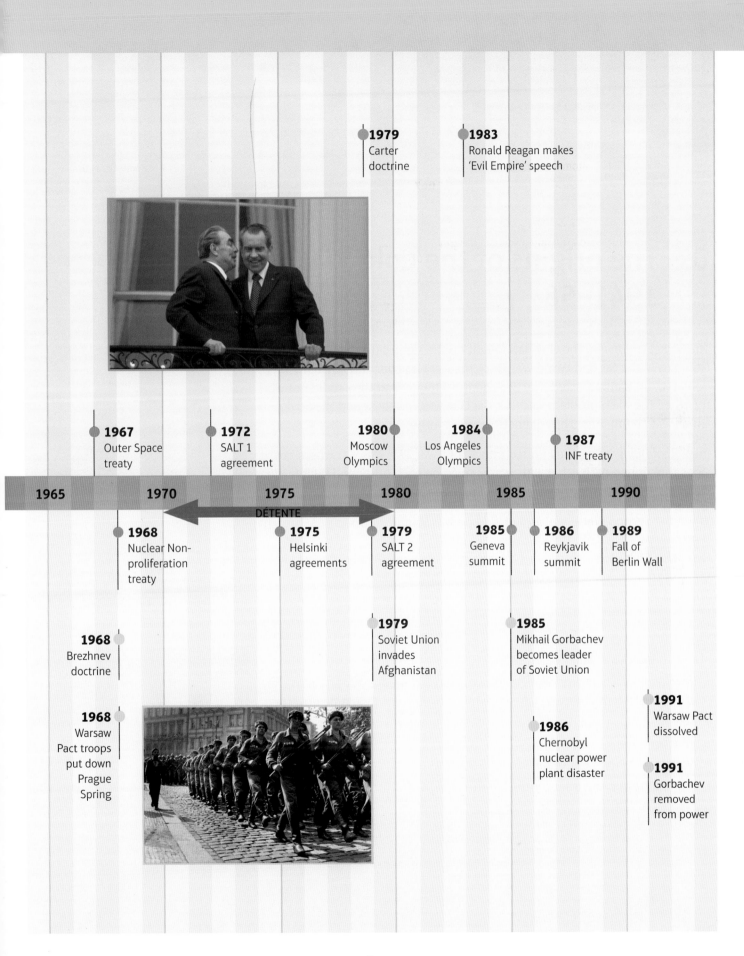

1979
Carter doctrine

1983
Ronald Reagan makes 'Evil Empire' speech

1967
Outer Space treaty

1972
SALT 1 agreement

1980
Moscow Olympics

1984
Los Angeles Olympics

1987
INF treaty

| 1965 | 1970 | 1975 | 1980 | 1985 | 1990 |

DÉTENTE

1968
Nuclear Non-proliferation treaty

1975
Helsinki agreements

1979
SALT 2 agreement

1985
Geneva summit

1986
Reykjavik summit

1989
Fall of Berlin Wall

1968
Brezhnev doctrine

1979
Soviet Union invades Afghanistan

1985
Mikhail Gorbachev becomes leader of Soviet Union

1991
Warsaw Pact dissolved

1968
Warsaw Pact troops put down Prague Spring

1986
Chernobyl nuclear power plant disaster

1991
Gorbachev removed from power

01 | The origins of the Cold War, 1941–58

The Soviet Union and the USA had fought on the same side against Hitler's Germany in the Second World War. Once the war was over and Germany was defeated, problems started. The two countries found that they could not work together. The main problem was that the USA was capitalist and the Soviet Union was communist. They did not trust each other.

Instead of being allies, they drifted into a 'cold' war. This was war where both sides threatened each other with words, spied on each other and built nuclear weapons. However, they never actually fought each other.

When the Second World War ended, Europe was split into two halves. The West was capitalist and the East was communist, controlled by the Soviet Red Army. The Soviet Union tried to strengthen its control in Europe while the USA tried to weaken the control the Soviet Union had over eastern European countries.

Learning outcomes

In this chapter you will find out:

- how ideological differences helped bring about the Cold War and how they affected attempts to reach agreement on how Europe should be governed
- how US / Soviet rivalry in the years 1947–49 led to the division of Europe into 'two camps'
- how the development of the atomic bomb led to an arms race
- how opposition to Soviet control led to an unsuccessful uprising in Hungary.

1.1 Early tensions between East and West

During the Second World War, the Soviet Union*, the USA and Britain were allies fighting against Nazi Germany. Britain's prime minister, Winston Churchill, nicknamed this alliance 'The Grand Alliance'. As soon as it became clear that Hitler would be defeated, tension and rivalry between the Soviet Union and the other allies began to grow. This became the Cold War*.

Ideological differences between East and West

The Soviet Union, Britain and the USA were ruled according to very different ideologies*. Britain and the USA were capitalist*. The Soviet Union was communist*.

Key terms

Political outlook*

The way a government believes their country should be run.

Soviet Union*

Known as the USSR. It was a group of communist countries. It was controlled by Russia.

Ideology*

A set of shared beliefs. In 1941, the USA and the Soviet Union had different ideologies concerning how a country should be run.

Capitalism*

Capitalists believe everyone should be free to own property and businesses and make money. The USA was a capitalist country.

Communism*

Communists believe that all property, including homes and businesses, should belong to the state, to ensure that every member of society has a fair share. The Soviet Union was communist.

Timeline

East–West relations, 1941–49

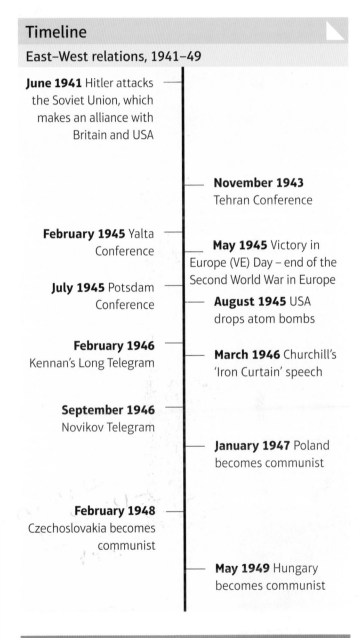

June 1941 Hitler attacks the Soviet Union, which makes an alliance with Britain and USA

November 1943 Tehran Conference

February 1945 Yalta Conference

May 1945 Victory in Europe (VE) Day – end of the Second World War in Europe

July 1945 Potsdam Conference

August 1945 USA drops atom bombs

February 1946 Kennan's Long Telegram

March 1946 Churchill's 'Iron Curtain' speech

September 1946 Novikov Telegram

January 1947 Poland becomes communist

February 1948 Czechoslovakia becomes communist

May 1949 Hungary becomes communist

Key term

Cold War*

A war where the sides threaten each other but do not actually fight.

Differences between leaders

Roosevelt, Churchill and Stalin (the leaders of the USA, Britain and the Soviet Union in 1941) are often called 'the Big Three'. Churchill and Roosevelt did not trust Stalin, and he did not trust them. The differences in the leaders' personal political beliefs were a major factor in the breakdown of relations as the Second World War ended.

Differences between nations

During the 1930s, both the USA and Britain had criticised the way in which Stalin had tried to turn the Soviet Union into an industrialised country. Many people had died in the process. However, Stalin was a strong opponent of Germany and so the USA and Britain needed to work with the Soviet Union to defeat Hitler. Once the war came to an end, however, the ideological differences between them meant it was impossible to agree on how post-war Europe should be governed.

Summary of the differences between the Soviet Union and the West

	Soviet Union	USA and Britain
Politics	Only one party	Free elections with a choice of parties
Social structure	Everyone is equal	Some people have more power than others (because of family background or wealth)
Economy	All property owned by the state, not individuals	Private ownership of property
Rights	Not many individual rights	More individual freedoms

Franklin D. Roosevelt
President of the USA: 1933-45
He believed strongly in democracy. He did not trust Stalin but he was not always as tough in negotiations* with Stalin as Churchill would have liked. Roosevelt believed any long-term settlement would only be possible if the Soviet Union was accepted as a superpower*.

Key terms

Negotiations*

When leaders of different countries meet to discuss an issue.

Superpower*

A country which is unusually strong and influences other countries. The USA and the Soviet Union were both superpowers.

Winston Churchill
Prime minister of Britain: 1940-45, 1951-55

Churchill did not trust Stalin. He saw his role as trying to stop the Soviet Union from taking control of eastern Europe.

Joseph Stalin
Leader of the Soviet Union: 1920s-1953

Stalin strengthened communist rule in the Soviet Union. He believed that the West wanted to destroy communism, so the Soviet Union had to stand firm in any negotiations with the Western 'superpower', the USA, and its close ally, Britain.

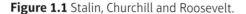

Figure 1.1 Stalin, Churchill and Roosevelt.

Figure 1.2 US and Soviet thinking after the Second World War.

A new world order

The Second World War changed world politics. The 'old powers', like Britain and France, were now less important than they had been. Two new 'superpowers', the Soviet Union and the USA had replaced them. Their military and economic strength were responsible for the defeat of Germany but their strength also made the Soviet Union and the USA rivals.

The Grand Alliance

In the Second World War, the Grand Alliance was formed between the USA, the Soviet Union and Britain to defeat Germany and Japan. Although the three countries had formed an alliance*, there was no real change in how they viewed each other. The USA and Britain, in particular, distrusted communism, and Stalin realised that the West would not want to take any actions that made the Soviet Union stronger in the long run.

The leaders of The Grand Alliance nations met three times during the war: at Tehran (1943), Yalta (February 1945) and Potsdam (July 1945).

Figure: The Grand Alliance conferences, 1943–45

Tehran Conference	Yalta Conference	Potsdam Conference
November 1943 Middle of Second World War	February 1945 Near end of Second World War	July–August 1945 After Germany surrendered

> **Key terms**
>
> **Democracy***
> A political system in which a nation's leaders are chosen in free elections.
>
> **Satellite state***
> Countries that came under the control of the Soviet Union after the Second World War.
>
> **Alliance***
> When two or more countries agree to work together.

> **Key term**
>
> **Second front***
> This was Stalin's demand that Britain and the USA should invade Europe to make Germany fight on two sides.

The significance of the Tehran, Yalta and Potsdam conferences

Tehran, November 1943
The Grand Alliance first met in Tehran to plan a winning strategy to end the war.

Who was at Tehran?	Why did they have the meeting?	What did they want?
Roosevelt (USA) Churchill (Britain) Stalin (Soviet Union)	The three countries wanted to agree how they would work together to fight Nazi Germany.	• Stalin wanted Britain and the USA to open a 'second front'* to fight Germany in Europe. • The USA wanted the Soviet Union to help it to fight Japan.

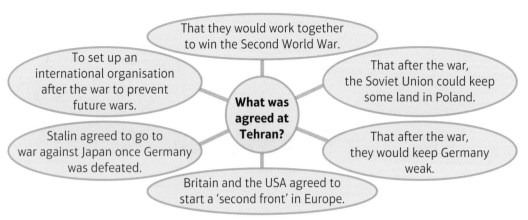

Figure: The Tehran agreement, 1943.

Stalin was pleased that Britain and the USA had agreed to open a 'second front' as this would help the Soviet Union, but there were tensions between Britain and the USA. Churchill had wanted to open the 'second front' in the Balkans*, but Roosevelt had agreed with Stalin that it would be in the West.

Key terms

Balkans*

Area in south-eastern Europe, including modern Albania, Bulgaria, Serbia and other countries.

Reparations*

Payments after a war from the losing country to the victors. Reparations are compensation for loss of life and damage to land and the economy.

United Nations*

An international organisation set up in 1945. Its aim was to keep peace around the world.

Yalta, February 1945

The Grand Alliance met two years later at Yalta.

Who was at Yalta?	Why did they have the meeting?	What did they want?
Roosevelt (USA) Churchill (Britain) Stalin (Soviet Union)	• The 'second front' was pushing back German troops towards Berlin. The Soviet troops had defeated the German invasion of Russia and were also pushing back the German Army. • The allies wanted to talk about winning the war and how they would run Europe after the war.	• Stalin wanted to make sure that he kept control of parts of Eastern Europe at the end of the war. • Britain and the USA wanted to make sure that there was peace in Europe.

The leaders at Yalta and Tehran were the same.

Germany would be split into four zones, each run by one of the allies (Britain, France, the USA and the Soviet Union).

Stalin could keep parts of Poland, but Poland would be a free country with free elections.

Germany would pay $20 billion in reparations* for war damage.

Countries in Eastern Europe would have free elections.

What was agreed at Yalta?

Half the reparations would go to the Soviet Union as it had suffered the most.

Stalin agreed to join the war against Japan once Germany was defeated.

Germany's Nazi Party would be banned. Nazis who were caught would be tried as war criminals.

The United Nations* would be set up. It would start in 1945.

Figure: The Yalta agreement, 1945.

Roosevelt and Stalin were very pleased to have got an agreement over free elections and the United Nations. But Poland was a difficult topic and neither side was really happy. Stalin thought that Poland should become communist, but Britain and the USA wanted a free democratic government in Poland. It would be a problem in the future.

Source A

A photograph showing the Big Three – Winston Churchill, Franklin Roosevelt and Josef Stalin – at the Yalta conference in February 1945.

Postdam, July–August 1945

The Grand Alliance met a few months later at Potsdam.

Who was at Potsdam?	Why did they have the meeting?	What did they want?
Truman (USA) Attlee (Britain) Stalin (Soviet Union)	• Germany had surrendered. The Allies needed to finalise their agreement on how to run Europe.	• Stalin wanted to make sure that the Soviet Union remained powerful in Eastern Europe. • Truman wanted to have peace in Europe but also prevent communism spreading. • Attlee wanted to finish the conferences quickly and return to Britain.

The USA and Britain had new leaders for this meeting.

The Potsdam Conference was different from the earlier conferences for several important reasons:

1 There were different leaders. Stalin was more experienced than Truman and Attlee, so it was harder for them to get their way.

2 The USA had built an atomic bomb, which it tested at the start of the conference. This meant that the Soviet Union didn't trust the USA and in fact was jealous of it.

3 The United Nations had been created. The Big Three – the USA, the Soviet Union and Britain – were all important members.

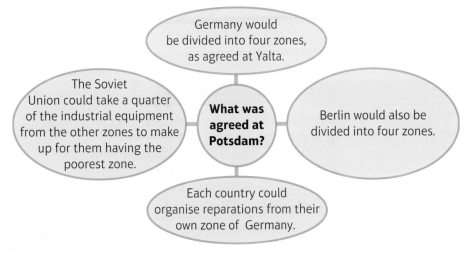

Figure: The Potsdam agreement, 1945.

By the summer of 1945, the Big Three had agreed on some major things, but there were some things that they had not agreed.

1. Truman wanted the Soviet Red Army to leave the Eastern European countries that they had freed from Nazi Germany. Stalin wanted to keep the soldiers there.

2. Truman was unhappy that the Soviet Union was going to keep some land in Poland. This had been agreed at the earlier Yalta Conference.

Figure 1.3 The post-war division of Germany into four parts: the Soviet, French, British and American zones.

Exam-style question, Section A

Explain **two** consequences of the decisions made by The Grand Alliance at the Yalta Conference in February 1945. **8 marks**

Exam tip

The question asks about 'consequences'. This means what changed because of the event. Don't just tell the story of what happened, explain why the decision was important. What was different? For example, it was agreed that Germany should be divided into four zones. How did that **affect** international relations? (See pages 97–98 for examples of answers to the question.)

Activities ?

1. Copy this table and complete the blank boxes.

	Who was there?	What are three things they agreed on?	Did it make relations between the 'Big Three' better or worse? Give one reason.
Tehran, 1943	Churchill Roosevelt Stalin		
Yalta, 1945		1 To split Germany into four zones 2 Germany to pay reparations 3 Eastern Europe to have free elections	
Potsdam, 1945			

2. Discuss in your group what things the Big Three did not agree on. Which of these do you think would cause the most problems in the future?

3. Give one reason for your group's choice.

US–Soviet relations 1945–46: the wartime alliance unravels

Although the members of The Grand Alliance agreed on many issues at the Tehran, Yalta and Potsdam conferences, by the end of Postdam, it was clear that there were now important issues that they could not agree on. Stalin wanted control of Eastern Europe to protect the Soviet Union. But Truman believed that Stalin was trying to spread communism. In the years 1945–46, this disagreement and lack of trust turned the wartime alliance into peacetime hostility.

The impact of the atom bomb on US–Soviet relations

Although Germany had been defeated, the war against Japan continued. On 6 August 1945, the USA exploded an atomic bomb over the Japanese city of Hiroshima. A second was released over Nagasaki on 9 August. It is estimated that over 120,000 Japanese civilians were killed by the bombs.

Some historians argue that the USA could have won the war against Japan without using nuclear weapons. They say the USA used the bombs to show that it was stronger than the Soviet Union. This is only an opinion, but it is true that knowing the USA could make atomic bombs gave Truman more confidence to negotiate at Potsdam.

Because of the atomic bomb, Stalin was determined to make the Soviet Union secure. His immediate aim was to create a buffer zone* of countries that supported communism between Germany and the Soviet Union's western borders.

Soviet scientists were already working on their own version of the atomic bomb and their first successful test was in 1949.

The bomb made Cold War tensions between the USA and the Soviet Union much worse. A war that used atomic weapons could kill millions of people. But, equally, the dangers of using an atomic bomb made both the USA and the Soviet Union try to avoid war. Instead they began an arms race, in which each side tried to make sure their nuclear weapons were more powerful than those of their rival.

Key terms

Buffer zone*

The Eastern European countries which the Soviet Union controlled acted as a barrier to protect the Soviet Union.

Embassies*

Countries send representatives to other countries to take part in negotiations.

Activities ?

1 Look at Source B. It is called 'The Big Fourth'.
   a Who were the Big Three?
   b In the cartoon, what is the 'Big Fourth'?
   c In a small group discuss why the cartoon is called 'The Big Fourth'.

2 This cartoon was published in July 1945. If Zec had drawn it on 10 August, how might it have been different? Draw your own version.

Source B

This cartoon, 'The Big Fourth', by the British cartoonist Philip Zec, was published in the *Daily Mirror* on 17 July 1945.

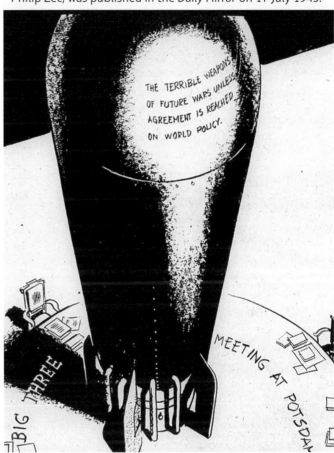

Rising tensions: the Kennan Long Telegram and the Novikov Telegram

Both Truman and Stalin feared that the break-up of The Grand Alliance might lead to another war. They wanted to know what their rivals were thinking and, in 1946, both asked their embassies* to report on attitudes in each other's countries. These reports came in the form of telegrams – a written message sent over a telegraph line.

Source C

From the 'Long Telegram' sent from Moscow to Washington by the US ambassador to the Soviet Union, George Kennan, on 22 February 1946.

We have here a political force committed fanatically to the belief that... it is desirable and necessary that... our traditional way of life be destroyed, the international authority of our state be broken, if Soviet power is to be secure... But... the problem is within our power to solve... without... military conflict.

Key terms

Ambassador*

A representative of a country who lives in another country. Their job is to speak for their country in meetings with other governments and to send messages back to their own government.

Containment*

The US policy of stopping communism spreading.

Satellite states*

Countries that came under the control of the Soviet Union after the Second World War.

Domination*

When a strong country influences or controls other countries and tells them what to do.

Imperialism*

When a country believes it has the right to have an empire and control other countries.

Soviet attitudes: George Kennan's Long Telegram

George Kennan, the US ambassador* in Moscow, sent a telegram (see Source C, page 15) discussing US–Soviet relations. His views were taken seriously by the US government. Most telegrams were very short, but Kennan's telegram was long, so his message became known as the Long Telegram. It contained a message that worried the US government.

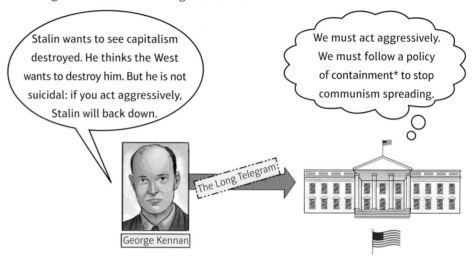

US attitudes: the Novikov Telegram

Nikolai Novikov was the Soviet ambassador working in Washington. His telegram to the government in Moscow shows that the Soviet Union thought equally poorly of the West: each side distrusted the other.

Source D

From the 'Novikov Telegram' sent from Washington to Moscow by Nikolai Novikov, Soviet Ambassador to the USA, on 27 September 1946.

US foreign policy has been characterized in the postwar period by a desire for world domination*. All these steps to preserve the great military potential are not an end in itself, of course. They are intended only to prepare conditions to win world domination in a new war being planned by the most warlike circles of American imperialism*...

Source E

From a speech given by Winston Churchill on 5 March 1946 at Westminster College, Fulton, Missouri. Here he describes the Soviet Union's growing control over Eastern Europe.

From Stettin in the Baltic to Trieste in the Adriatic, an iron curtain has descended across the Continent. Behind that line lie all the capitals of the ancient states of Central and Eastern Europe... all are subject in one form or another, not only to Soviet influence but to a very high and, in some cases, increasing measure of control from Moscow.

A British point-of-view: Winston Churchill's 'Iron Curtain' speech

In March 1946, Winston Churchill gave a speech, which made it plain that he thought the Soviet Union was a threat to freedom and world peace. He said this because communist governments had recently been set up in Hungary, Poland, Romania and Bulgaria, which became satellite states of the Soviet Union.

Churchill was speaking in the USA, so Stalin thought the Americans had the same beliefs as Churchill. The speech, along with the Novikov Telegram, increased tension and mistrust and caused the Soviet Union to strengthen its forces. Churchill's speech increased the growing hostility between East and West.

The creation of Soviet satellite states in Eastern Europe

In 1944 and 1945, the Soviet Red Army freed many countries in Eastern Europe from the Nazis. When the war was over, Stalin did not want to give up control of these countries as they were a useful buffer zone between the Soviet Union and Germany. He turned them into satellite states with communist governments. Truman saw this as evidence that the Soviet Union wanted to spread communism worldwide. The relationship between the USA and the Soviet Union became worse.

Source F

A photograph of Klement Gottwald speaking at a communist rally in Prague, February 1948. After a coalition* government collapsed, Gottwald became president of a communist Czechoslovakia.

Activities ?

1 What term does Churchill use in his speech (Source E) to describe the imaginary line between East and West in Europe?

2 In a small group, re-read Sources C, D and E and discuss what they mean. Together, decide on a one or two sentence explanation of what each writer was saying.

3 In your group, half will represent the USA and half will represent the the Soviet Union. Your job will be to say that the worsening relations after 1941 were not your country's fault, but all the other side's fault.

   a Write down three reasons that you can use to blame the other side for international relations getting worse.

   b Taking it in turns, someone on each side needs to give a reason why it is the other side's fault.

   c At the end, decide whether you would blame the USA, the Soviet Union, or both.

Key term

Coalition*

When a single political party doesn't have enough support to form a government, several parties can join together in a coalition and form a coalition government.

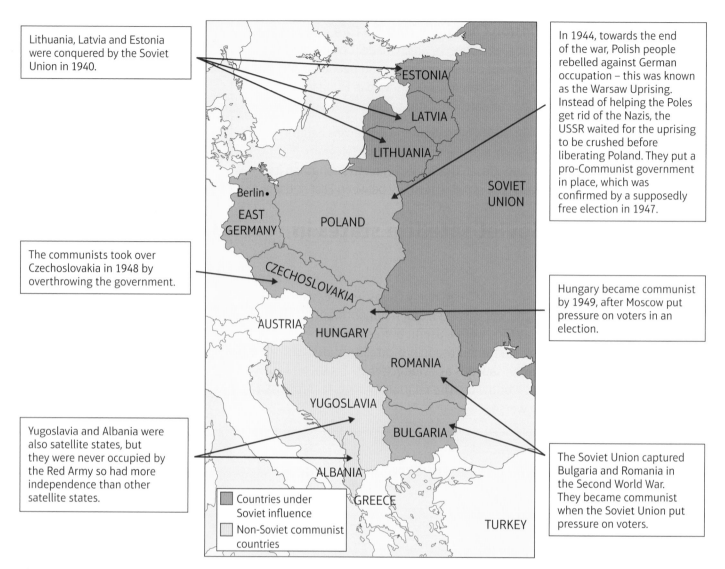

Lithuania, Latvia and Estonia were conquered by the Soviet Union in 1940.

In 1944, towards the end of the war, Polish people rebelled against German occupation – this was known as the Warsaw Uprising. Instead of helping the Poles get rid of the Nazis, the USSR waited for the uprising to be crushed before liberating Poland. They put a pro-Communist government in place, which was confirmed by a supposedly free election in 1947.

The communists took over Czechoslovakia in 1948 by overthrowing the government.

Hungary became communist by 1949, after Moscow put pressure on voters in an election.

Yugoslavia and Albania were also satellite states, but they were never occupied by the Red Army so had more independence than other satellite states.

The Soviet Union captured Bulgaria and Romania in the Second World War. They became communist when the Soviet Union put pressure on voters.

Countries under Soviet influence
Non-Soviet communist countries

Figure 1.4 How the countries of Eastern Europe became Soviet satellite states.

Major events 1941–46

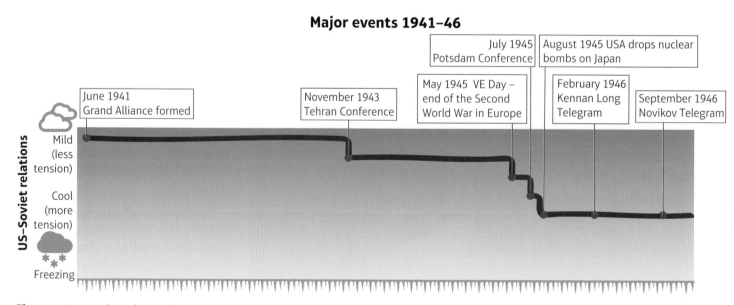

July 1945 Potsdam Conference

August 1945 USA drops nuclear bombs on Japan

June 1941 Grand Alliance formed

November 1943 Tehran Conference

May 1945 VE Day – end of the Second World War in Europe

February 1946 Kennan Long Telegram

September 1946 Novikov Telegram

US–Soviet relations

Mild (less tension)

Cool (more tension)

Freezing

Figure 1.5 How the relationship between the USA and the Soviet Union worsened, 1941–46.

Exam-style question, Section A

Write a narrative account analysing the key events of the Soviet takeover of the satellite states in the period 1944–48.

You may use the following in your answer:

- the Warsaw Uprising
- the communist takeover of Czechoslovakia.

You **must** also use information of your own.   **8 marks**

Exam tip

This type of question is looking for the story – a narrative account – of the events. You need to show that you know what the event is about, and that you can connect the main parts.

To answer this question, ask yourself: Why did the event happen? What happened? What were the results of the event?

Summary

- Although they followed different ideologies, from 1941 to 1945 the USA, the Soviet Union and Britain were allies against a common enemy, Nazi Germany.
- In 1943, the Big Three began talks (at Tehran) about how to end the war and how to deal with Germany after the war. Final agreement on the division of Germany into four zones of occupation came at Yalta in 1945.
- Victory in Europe (VE) Day saw Allied victory over Nazi Germany and left the Soviet Red Army in control of what became the satellite states: Poland, Czechoslovakia, Bulgaria, Romania, Hungary, Yugoslavia and the Soviet zone of Germany.
- In August 1945, the USA exploded two atomic bombs over Japan. From now on, international relations were affected by these powerful new weapons.
- By 1946, the USA and the Soviet Union had lost trust in each other. Both believed that their countries' ideologies were under threat because of the aggressive foreign policies of each other.

Checkpoint

Strengthen

S1 What is a cold war?

S2 Which leaders attended the Tehran and Potsdam conferences?

S3 What did the Allies plan for Germany at Yalta? Is this what finally happened?

S4 In your own words, explain the differences between communism and capitalism.

Challenge

C1 How did the invention of the atomic bomb affect East–West relations?

How confident do you feel about your answers to these questions? Form a small group and discuss any questions you are not sure about. Look for the answers in this section. Now rewrite your answers as a group.

1.2 The development of the Cold War

Timeline

Growing East–West divisions, 1947–49

March 1947 Truman puts forward the Truman Doctrine

June 1947 Marshall Aid plan announced

September 1947 First Cominform meeting

February 1948 Czechoslovakia becomes communist

June 1948 Berlin blockade is set up

January 1949 Comecon set up

April 1949 NATO formed

September 1949 FDR (West Germany) created

October 1949 GDR (East Germany) created

May 1955 Warsaw Pact formed

Key term

US Congress*

Part of the American government.

The impact of the Truman Doctrine and Marshall Plan

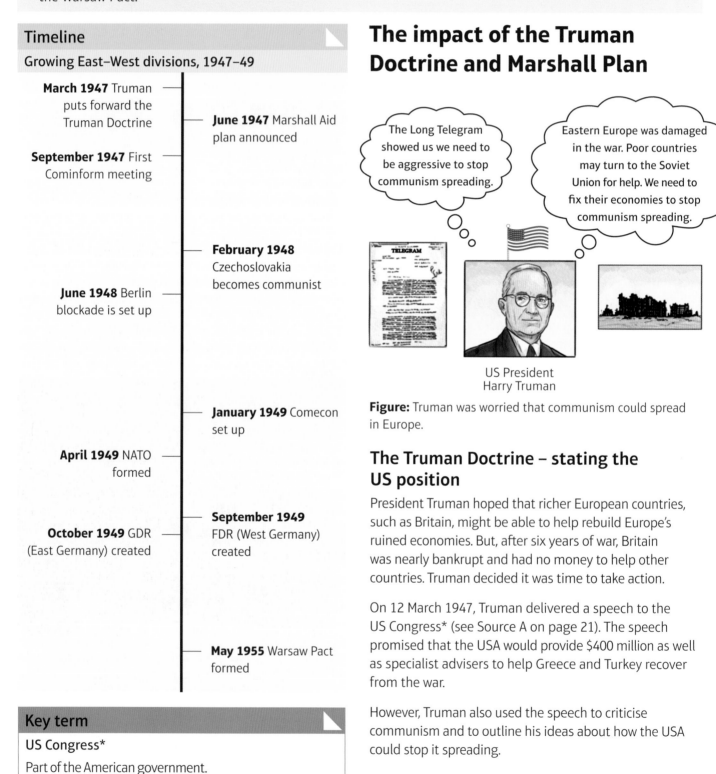

The Long Telegram showed us we need to be aggressive to stop communism spreading.

Eastern Europe was damaged in the war. Poor countries may turn to the Soviet Union for help. We need to fix their economies to stop communism spreading.

US President Harry Truman

Figure: Truman was worried that communism could spread in Europe.

The Truman Doctrine – stating the US position

President Truman hoped that richer European countries, such as Britain, might be able to help rebuild Europe's ruined economies. But, after six years of war, Britain was nearly bankrupt and had no money to help other countries. Truman decided it was time to take action.

On 12 March 1947, Truman delivered a speech to the US Congress* (see Source A on page 21). The speech promised that the USA would provide $400 million as well as specialist advisers to help Greece and Turkey recover from the war.

However, Truman also used the speech to criticise communism and to outline his ideas about how the USA could stop it spreading.

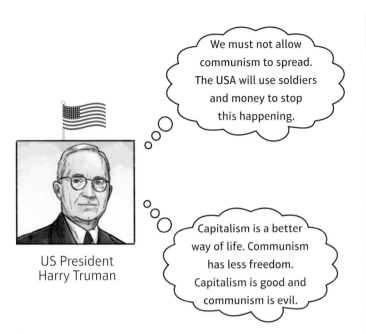

Figure: The Truman Doctrine.

Truman's ideas became known as 'the Truman Doctrine'. Before the Second World War, the USA had followed a policy of isolationism*. This policy was now abandoned. The USA was setting itself up as the leader of the fight against communism. Isolationism was replaced with a policy of containment* in the USA.

Source A

From the Truman Doctrine speech delivered on 12 March 1947 to the US Congress. Immediately before this extract, Truman described American-style democracy as majority rule* and freedom from political oppression*.

The second way of life is based upon the will of a minority forcibly imposed upon the majority. It relies upon terror and oppression, a controlled press and radio; fixed elections, and the suppression of personal freedoms. I believe that our help should be primarily through economic and financial aid* which is essential to economic stability and orderly political processes.

Key term

Isolationism*

Staying apart, not getting involved in the affairs of others. The USA followed a policy of isolationism until the Second World War. When the war ended, many Americans hoped the country would return to isolationism.

Key terms

Infrastructure*

Things like roads, railways, schools, hospitals, electricity grids and phone networks, which help a country function.

Containment*

The US policy of stopping communism from spreading.

Majority rule*

A system, like democracy, where most people have a say in who runs the country.

Political oppression*

When a government keeps tight control to stop people disagreeing with it politically.

Economic and financial aid*

Helping countries to rebuild their economy by giving them money.

The Marshall Plan – fighting communism with financial aid

Source B

A photograph of American and British officials watching Caribbean sugar, sent under the Marshall Plan, being unloaded at Woolwich Docks.

The USA had not suffered damage to its infrastructure* and industry during the war in the same way as European countries had. Three months after Truman's speech, the US secretary of state, George Marshall, gave a speech saying that the USA would send aid to Europe.

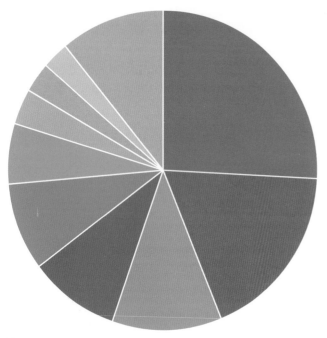

Key

- United Kingdom $3,297 million
- France $2,296 million
- West Germany $1,448 million
- Italy $1,204 million
- Netherlands $1,128 million
- Belgium & Luxembourg $777 million
- Austria $468 million
- Denmark $385 million
- Greece $376 million
- Other nations $1,352 million

Figure 1.6 The money given to European nations under the Marshall Plan was shared out according to population and how industrialised each country was before the war.

The Marshall Plan was a practical outcome of the Truman Doctrine: providing economic aid to help war-torn countries in Europe. The aim was to stop communism from spreading, as communism seemed attractive to people who had nothing. Between 1948 and 1952, the USA gave $12.7 billion dollars of aid.

The economic impact of Marshall Aid in Western Europe was enormous. The British foreign secretary, Ernest Bevin, called it 'a lifeline to sinking men'.

Money was offered to the Soviet Union and the satellite states, although countries would first have to agree to a review of their finances. The USA knew Stalin would not allow this so, in practice, Eastern European countries did not benefit from the Marshall Plan.

Source C

From a speech made by US Secretary of State, George Marshall, on 5 June 1947. Marshall said Europe could not possibly meet its own needs for food and essential products for the next three–four years and needed substantial help.

Our policy is directed not against any country or doctrine but against hunger, poverty, desperation and chaos. Its purpose should be the revival of a working economy in the world so as to permit the emergence of political and social conditions in which free institutions can exist...

Extend your knowledge

More about Marshall Aid
Marshall Aid was not just loans and grants of money to European governments. It also involved giving money to help groups in need. So it included nets for Norwegian fishermen, mules for Greek farmers and food for starving people.

'Dollar imperialism' – the Soviet response

President Truman saw his new policy as a way to contain communism. Not surprisingly, Stalin did not see it like that at all. He believed the Truman Doctrine showed that the USA was trying to widen its influence in Europe. Stalin argued that the Marshall Plan was a way of using economic power to divide Europe in two and establish an American economic empire in Europe. The Soviets called this 'dollar imperialism'.

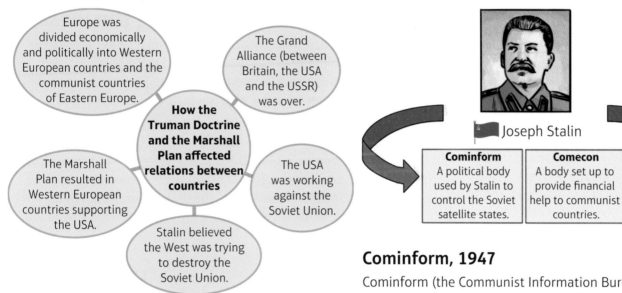

Figure: The Truman Doctrine and the Marshall Plan had a huge impact on international relations from 1947.

The formation of Cominform and Comecon

The Marshall Plan set Stalin an economic and political challenge. To meet this challenge, he set up two new organisations for the communist countries of Europe, Cominform and Comecon.

Key term

Propaganda*

When a government spreads a message to persuade people to believe something.

Cominform, 1947

Cominform (the Communist Information Bureau) was a political organisation set up on Stalin's orders in September 1947. It included the Communist Party of the Soviet Union, and the Communist Parties of the satellite states of Bulgaria, Czechoslovakia, Hungary, Poland and Romania along with Yugoslavia.

Cominform gave Stalin a way of directing and controlling the governments of the satellite states. They were encouraged to only trade with other Cominform members and not make contact with non-communist countries. This included not accepting Marshall Aid. Cominform spread anti-American propaganda*.

Comecon, 1949

Stalin knew that he needed to offer an alternative to Marshall Aid if he was to keep the satellite states under his control.

In January 1949, he set up Comecon (the Council for Mutual Economic Assistance) to provide aid to communist countries. Its members were the Soviet Union, Bulgaria, Czechoslovakia, Hungary, Poland, Romania and East Germany.

Comecon's main activities were arranging trade between member countries and encouraging industrial growth. Trade with the USA and Western Europe was discouraged in favour of trade with the Soviet Union and other member states.

Stalin set up Cominform and Comecon because he thought the Marshall Plan was a threat to the Soviet Union. But this increased tension. The USA and Western European countries created a new military alliance, the North Atlantic Treaty Organisation (NATO) in 1949.

The 1948 Berlin Crisis – testing the West

Europe was now divided into two political and economic camps*. These were the Western European countries – including Britain, France, Italy and Spain supported by the USA – and the USSR and the Eastern European communist states. Stalin wanted to see what the West would do if it was challenged.

Key terms

Camps*

Different, separate groups.

Military checkpoint*

A gateway where people could travel across the line between East and West. It was guarded by soldiers who checked who passed through.

Germany divided

At the Potsdam Conference in 1945, The Grand Alliance had agreed to divide Germany, and its capital Berlin, into four separate zones controlled by the Soviet Union, the USA, Britain and France. The division was meant to be temporary but lasted for many years. There were soldiers on the streets and, in Berlin, there were military checkpoints* between zones.

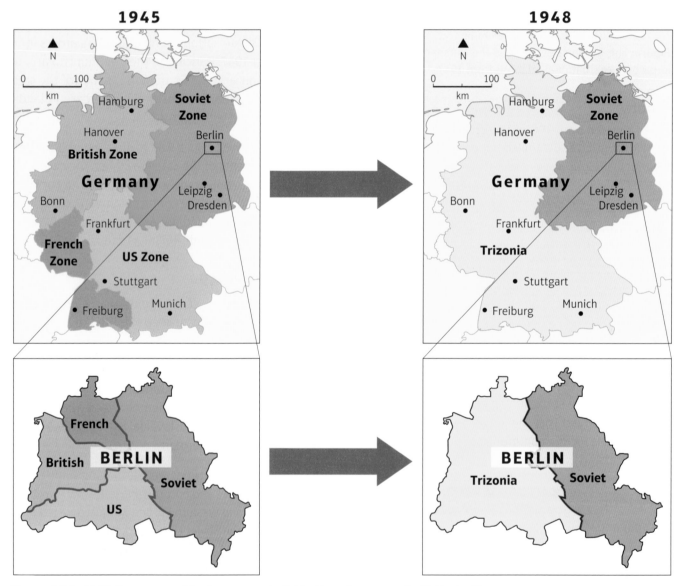

Figure 1.7 In 1945, Germany and Berlin were each divided into four zones. In 1948, the Western zones (French, British, US) were joined together to make Trizonia.

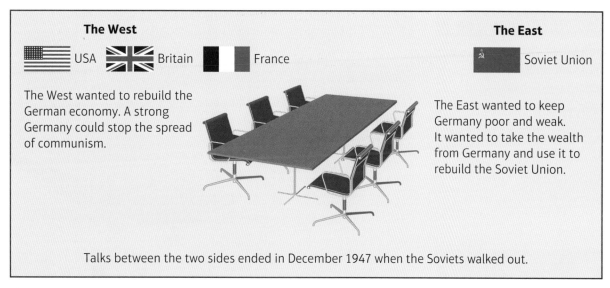

Figure: What the two sides wanted for Germany.

Uniting the Western zones

With the Soviets no longer co-operating, the remaining allies (the USA, Britain and France) had to decide how to run their parts of Germany. In March 1948, they combined their zones into one zone, 'Trizonia'. The result was that Germany and Berlin were now split into two parts, western Trizonia and eastern Soviet-controlled Germany.

Then, in June 1948, the three Allies created a single currency, the Deutschmark, which became the currency of Trizonia. The Soviets were furious about the decision for two reasons:

- The new single currency in Trizonia meant that Trizonia and the Soviet zone became two separate economic areas.
- It showed that there were two Germanys: West and East.

To Stalin, this was a further example of the West 'ganging up' on the Soviet Union. He was determined to make Germany one united country under communism.

The Berlin blockade

Stalin knew that the Western-occupied zones of Berlin were in a weak position because they were surrounded by Soviet-occupied territory.

In June 1948, Stalin decided to shut the land routes across Soviet-controlled Germany into Berlin, in what has become known as the 'Berlin blockade'. He wanted to show the USA, Britain and France that a divided Germany would not work. The people of Berlin would soon run short of food. If the blockade was successful, Stalin would win

a huge propaganda success. It might also mean that the Western powers would give up control of their zones in Berlin. The West could not get to Berlin by land without invading Soviet territory and risking war. Truman thought that the Allies could fly supplies in. He thought that Stalin would not be willing to risk war by shooting down a plane.

Operation Vittles: the Berlin Airlift

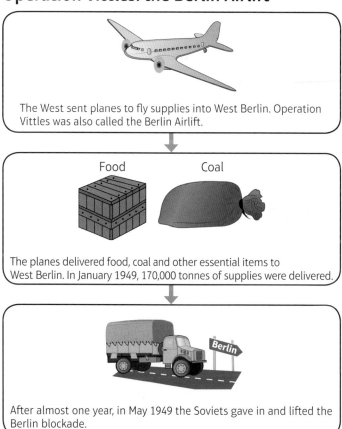

The West sent planes to fly supplies into West Berlin. Operation Vittles was also called the Berlin Airlift.

Food   Coal

The planes delivered food, coal and other essential items to West Berlin. In January 1949, 170,000 tonnes of supplies were delivered.

After almost one year, in May 1949 the Soviets gave in and lifted the Berlin blockade.

Figure: The Berlin Airlift.

Activities ?

1 Describe the Berlin Airlift in four sentences.

2 Give one reason why the USA was determined to keep the Western zones of Berlin out of Soviet hands.

3 In a small group, discuss what the results might have been if:

   a the Western Allies had not launched the Berlin Airlift.

   b Stalin had shot down the first planes flying supplies to Berlin.

The end of the Berlin blockade made the USA look stronger, as it had won without any casualties. The Soviet Union looked weak as it had backed down.

Source E

A photograph of children watching as a supply plane arrives in Berlin during the Berlin Airlift.

The formation of East and West Germany

After the Berlin blockade, it was clear that the division of Germany would continue. Britain, France and the USA quickly moved to create a separate West Germany.

Federal Republic of Germany (West Germany)

• May 1949: Just three days after the end of the blockade, the USA, Britain and France joined their zones together to become the Federal Republic of Germany. The new country became known as West Germany.

• August 1949: Germans in West Germany were allowed to elect their own parliament, called the *Bundestag*.

• The Federal Republic was much bigger than East Germany.

• The Western-controlled zones of Berlin became known as West Berlin.

German Democratic Republic (East Germany)

Stalin responded by creating the German Democratic Republic in October 1949. It became known as East Germany.

For the next 40 years, people would talk about West Germany and East Germany but, for most of this time, each German regarded their own state as the only real one.

The creation of two armed camps

NATO and the Warsaw Pact

Because they felt threatened, both the West and the East decided to set up their own military alliances.

	The North Atlantic Treaty Organisation (NATO) – The West	The Warsaw Pact – The East
When was it set up?	1949	1955
What was it?	A military alliance in the West. The members agreed that if any member was attacked, all of the other members would help them.	A military alliance in the East. The members agreed to defend each other in the case of a war.
Which countries were members?	• The USA • Britain • France Plus nine other Western countries	• The Soviet Union • Seven satellite states, including Poland, Czechoslovakia and Hungary
Why was it set up?	The Berlin Blockade had shown that there was a real danger of conflict with the Soviet Union. This alliance aimed to protect its members.	The creation of NATO worried the Soviet Union. When West Germany joined NATO, the Warsaw Pact was made a week later.
How did it affect international relations?	NATO showed that the West was prepared to use military force. It also meant that the USA kept soldiers in Europe. The Soviet Union felt threatened.	The Warsaw Pact was a threat to the West. It also showed that Europe was now completely divided in two militarily.

There was now no doubt that Europe was, in reality, two Europes. One was under the protection of the USA and working to defeat communism. The other was led by the Soviet Union and seeking to extend communist control. The hostility between these two camps would affect international relations for the next 35 years.

Source F

An extract from the NATO Charter*. Article 5 stated:

The Parties agree that an armed attack against one or more of them in Europe or North America shall be considered an attack against them all and consequently they agree that, if such an armed attack occurs, each of them... will assist the Party or Parties so attacked by taking such action as it deems necessary, including the use of armed force, to restore and maintain the security of the North Atlantic area.

Key term

Charter*
The rules that an organisation follows.

Activity ?

1 Make a list of all the important events that you can remember during the Cold War between 1947 and 1955.

2 Challenge a partner to see who can give the best one-minute speech about 'How the Cold War developed, 1947–55'. As you listen to your partner's speech, add any important events you think you have missed to your list.

Exam-style question, Section A

Explain **two** of the following:

- the importance of the Truman Doctrine for the development of the Cold War in the years 1947–55
- the importance of the Berlin Blockade for the future of Germany
- the importance of the formation of NATO for relations between the USA and the Soviet Union. **16 marks**

Exam tip

Remember that this question is not asking for a description of an event or policy. It is asking why that event or policy was important. What difference did it make? For example, the Truman Doctrine changed how the USA treated communist countries.

You could start with 'One way that the Truman Doctrine was important was...'

Remember to focus on the second part of each bullet point. For example, on the second bullet point, focus on the 'future of Germany'. You could mention how the blockade led to Germany becoming permanently divided into East and West Germany.

Summary

- In the Truman Doctrine, Truman promised to defend Western countries against communism.
- George Marshall, the US secretary of state, promised massive aid to Europe, launching the Marshall Plan.
- Western European countries welcomed the Marshall Plan, but Soviet-controlled countries were not allowed to accept aid. The Soviet Union set up Cominform and Comecon as rivals to the Marshall Plan.
- West Berlin was blockaded by the Soviet Union. Britain and the USA organised a successful airlift to send supplies to the city.
- The USA agreed to keep troops in Europe. The North Atlantic Treaty Organisation (NATO) was set up in 1949.
- The Western-controlled areas of Germany were merged to form Trizonia, which eventually became the Federal Republic of Germany (West Germany). The Soviet zone became the German Democratic Republic (East Germany).
- The Soviet Union set up a defensive military alliance for the communist countries of Eastern Europe, the Warsaw Pact, in 1955.

Checkpoint

Strengthen

S1 What was the Truman Doctrine?

S2 What was the role of Comecon?

S3 Describe the events of the Berlin Airlift.

Challenge

C1 Why did Stalin create Cominform and Comecon?

How confident do you feel about your answers to these questions? If you feel unsure, re-read the section then try again.

1.3 The Cold War intensifies

Learning outcomes

- Understand how the arms race between the USA and Soviet Union increased international tension.
- Know about the events of the Hungarian Uprising when the people of Hungary attempted to break free of Soviet rule.

By 1949, Europe was divided into two camps. This was mainly because there was disagreement about how to rule Germany.

The USA and the Soviet Union both wanted to be the more powerful, so they began a race to make bigger, better weapons.

The arms race: Soviet Union v. USA, 1950–58

After the USA had made the first atomic bomb in 1945, it felt safer because the bomb was more powerful than conventional* weapons.

By 1949, Stalin's scientists had made a Soviet atomic bomb. So, the USA developed the hydrogen bomb in 1952. This was 1,000 times more powerful than the atomic bomb. One year later, the Soviet Union also had a hydrogen bomb.

In 1957, the USA developed the ICBM (inter-continental ballistic missile), which could fire a nuclear warhead 4,500 kilometres. Soon, the Soviet Union also developed ICBMs.

The competition to build nuclear weapons became known as the arms race*.

Timeline

Cold War, 1950–58

November 1952 USA successfully tests hydrogen bomb

January 1953 Eisenhower becomes US President

March 1953 Stalin dies

August 1953 The Soviet Union successfully tests hydrogen bomb

May 1955 West Germany joins NATO

February 1956 Khrushchev, the new leader of the Soviet Union, makes a speech criticising Stalin

November 1956 Hungarian Uprising crushed

June 1957 USA launches first ICBM (inter-continental ballistic missile)

August 1957 Soviet Union tests first ICBM

June 1958 Imre Nagy, prime minister of Hungary, is executed

Key terms

Conventional*

Ordinary. Conventional weapons are any weapons that are not nuclear, chemical or biological.

Arms race*

When countries compete against each other to make more powerful weapons.

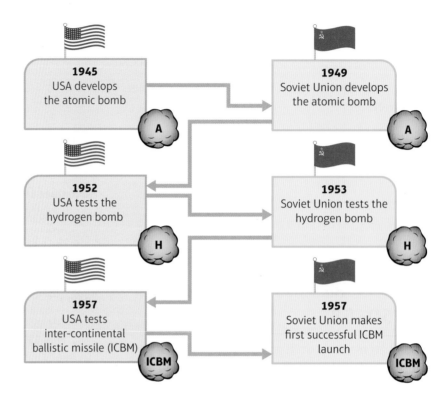

Figure 1.8 A timeline of the arms race.

Source A

A photograph of a US atom bomb test in the Pacific, in 1951.

Both the USA and the Soviet Union spent huge sums of money on building up large armies, navies, submarine fleets and stocks of conventional and nuclear missiles. It was important to try to stay ahead in the race and stop the other side becoming more powerful. However, the weapons that were being developed were so powerful that, from the early 1950s, both the USA and the Soviet Union could have destroyed the world many times over.

The USA and the Soviet Union could not risk fighting each other because their weapons were so powerful. The nuclear weapons acted as a deterrent*.

Key terms

Deterrent*

Something that stops one country from attacking another country.

Co-existence*

When two sides try to live peacefully without trying to destroy each other.

New leaders for the USA and the Soviet Union

Source B

A photograph of Nikita Khrushchev answering questions at a press conference in Paris in 1960.

New leaders

A new leader for the USA

Eisenhower was elected as president in 1952. He wanted to stop communism spreading, but he knew that nuclear war would be dangerous. He was willing to try to improve relations with the Soviet Union.

We should avoid nuclear war.

A new leader for the Soviet Union

Stalin died in 1953. **Khrushchev** became the new leader in 1956. He criticised the way Stalin had ruled the Soviet Union and said that there should be peaceful co-existence*.

We should have peaceful co-existence.

New thinking

End of the Korean War

There had been a war in Korea since 1950. The USA and the Soviet Union had been supporting different sides. But the fighting stopped in 1953.

Cut spending

The USA and the Soviet Union were spending lots of money on nuclear weapons. Both sides knew they would be better off if they spent less on weapons.

Agreements

In 1955, the USA and the Soviet Union met in Geneva to discuss how to run Germany and how to cut the number of nuclear weapons. Even though they did not reach an agreement, the two sides showed they could work together.

Key terms

Uprising*

When the people in a country become so unhappy that they rebel against the government.

Political freedom*

Able to share your opinions about the government without the risk of arrest.

Free elections*

Able to vote for more than one political party. In communist countries, the people could only vote for the Communist Party.

Freedom of speech*

Able to say or write what you want without being arrested by the government.

Unfortunately, better relations between the USA and the Soviet Union were only short-lived. In May 1955, West Germany joined NATO and the Soviet Union formed the Warsaw Pact. So the meeting in Geneva took place at a time when suspicion was still growing overall.

The Hungarian Uprising*, 1956

During 1956, the people of Hungary began to protest about their lack of political freedom* and problems such as fuel and food shortages. There were riots and police fought with protesters.

Soviet troops ended the riots. Khrushchev approved a new prime minister, Imre Nagy. He was popular, and Khrushchev hoped this would end the protests.

Nagy immediately put forward new laws. He wanted to include non-communist politicians in his government. He also set free many political prisoners and got Khrushchev to remove the Soviet troops from Hungary.

Khrushchev was ready to accept these changes if they ended the unrest in Hungary.

Timeline
The Hungarian Uprising, 1956

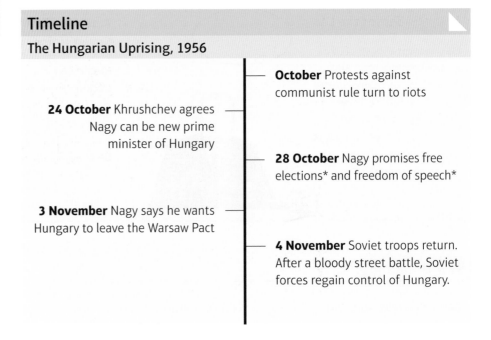

October Protests against communist rule turn to riots

24 October Khrushchev agrees Nagy can be new prime minister of Hungary

28 October Nagy promises free elections* and freedom of speech*

3 November Nagy says he wants Hungary to leave the Warsaw Pact

4 November Soviet troops return. After a bloody street battle, Soviet forces regain control of Hungary.

Khrushchev's response to the uprising

Nagy went too far with his new reforms. He said that he wanted Hungary to leave the Warsaw Pact. He thought Khrushchev would allow this because Khrushchev had previously criticised some of Stalin's policies. But Khrushchev could not risk losing one of his satellite states*. This would weaken the Soviet Union and make other satellite states think they could break away.

Khrushchev sent soldiers and 1,000 tanks into Hungary. Nagy's supporters fought back. Up to 20,000 Hungarians died in the fighting. No other countries helped Hungary despite urgent pleas for help from Nagy. Nagy was arrested and later executed.

Khrushchev set up a new, stronger communist government in Hungary with a new leader called Janos Kadar.

Source C

From a transcript* of Imre Nagy's last-minute plea for support as Soviet tanks rolled into Budapest on 4 November 1956.

This fight is the fight for freedom by the Hungarian people against the Russian [Soviet] intervention, and it is possible that I shall only be able to stay at my post for one or two hours. The whole world will see how the Russian armed forces, contrary to all treaties and conventions*, are crushing the resistance of the Hungarian people. I should like in these last moments to ask the leaders of the revolution, if they can, to leave the country... [For] today it is Hungary and tomorrow, or the day after tomorrow, it will be the turn of other countries, because the imperialism* of Moscow does not know borders and is only trying to play for time.

Extend your knowledge

Imre Nagy

Imre Nagy had sometimes disagreed with other parts of Hungary's Communist government and had been expelled twice. But he remained popular with the Hungarian people, and was therefore allowed to become Prime Minister in 1956 during the uprising.

When Soviet troops crushed Nagy's supporters, he was promised safe passage out of the country. But instead he was kidnapped by Soviet agents. He was tried and executed in 1958. Stalin described his death as 'a lesson to the leaders of all Socialist countries'.

Key terms

Satellite states*

The countries in Eastern Europe which the Soviet Union controlled.

Transcript*

A written record of a speech.

Treaties and conventions*

Agreements between different countries.

Imperialism*

When one country believes that it can invade and control another country.

Source D

A photograph of Hungarian rebels waving their national flag in Budapest, Hungary. They are standing on top of a captured Soviet tank.

Key term

Containment*

The US government's plan to stop communism spreading to countries that were not communist.

International reaction to the Soviet invasion of Hungary

When Nagy said that he wanted to leave the Warsaw Pact, his supporters in Hungary expected help from the USA. This was because:

- The US government had broadcast radio messages to the people in Eastern Europe calling on them to rise up against communism.
- The USA had offered Hungary money through the Marshall Plan. The Hungarian people thought the USA would support their uprising with soldiers too.
- Eisenhower agreed with the Hungarian Uprising.

But Nagy and the Hungarians were disappointed.

- The USA did not offer military help.
- The US policy of containment* meant the USA wanted to stop communism spreading. But it would not invade a communist country to do this as this would risk a nuclear war with the Soviet Union.

What was the impact of the Hungarian Uprising on international relations?

Khrushchev had shown he was a strong leader.

Members of the Warsaw Pact knew that they had to obey Khrushchev.

Communist countries knew the USA would not help them to leave the Warsaw Pact.

The Soviet Union was stronger than before.

Hungarian Uprising

The relationship between East and West was damaged.

The Soviet Union had shown it would use force to keep control of its satellite states.

The USA had encouraged a Warsaw Pact country to break away from the Soviet Union.

The reputation of the USA and the West was damaged.

Although the USA had encouraged the uprising, it did not help the Hungarians.

The USA had not sent Hungary any military support.

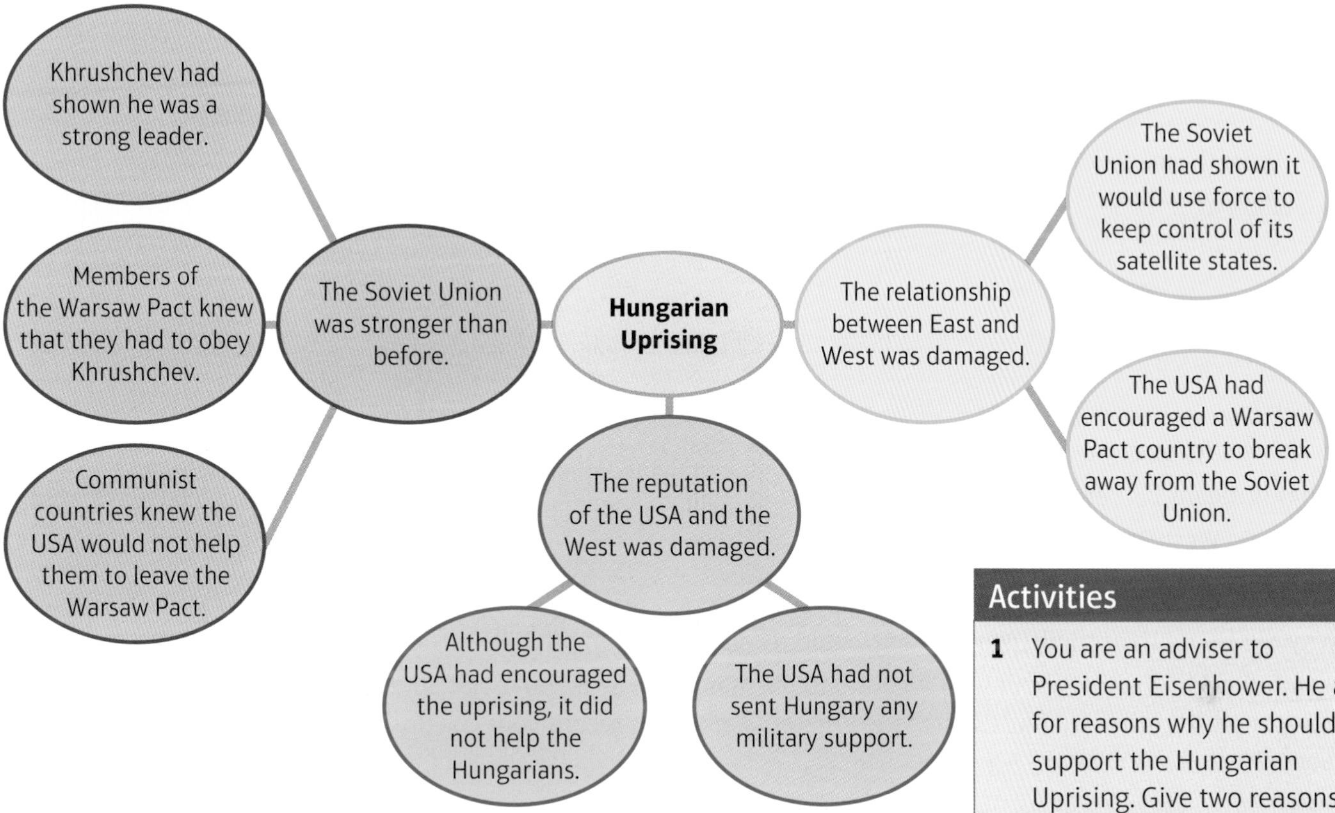

Figure: How the Hungarian Uprising affected international relations.

Activities ?

1 You are an adviser to President Eisenhower. He asks for reasons why he should support the Hungarian Uprising. Give two reasons.

2 President Eisenhower says he has received a report from another adviser with reasons why the USA should not intervene in Hungary. Give two reasons why the USA should not take part in the uprising.

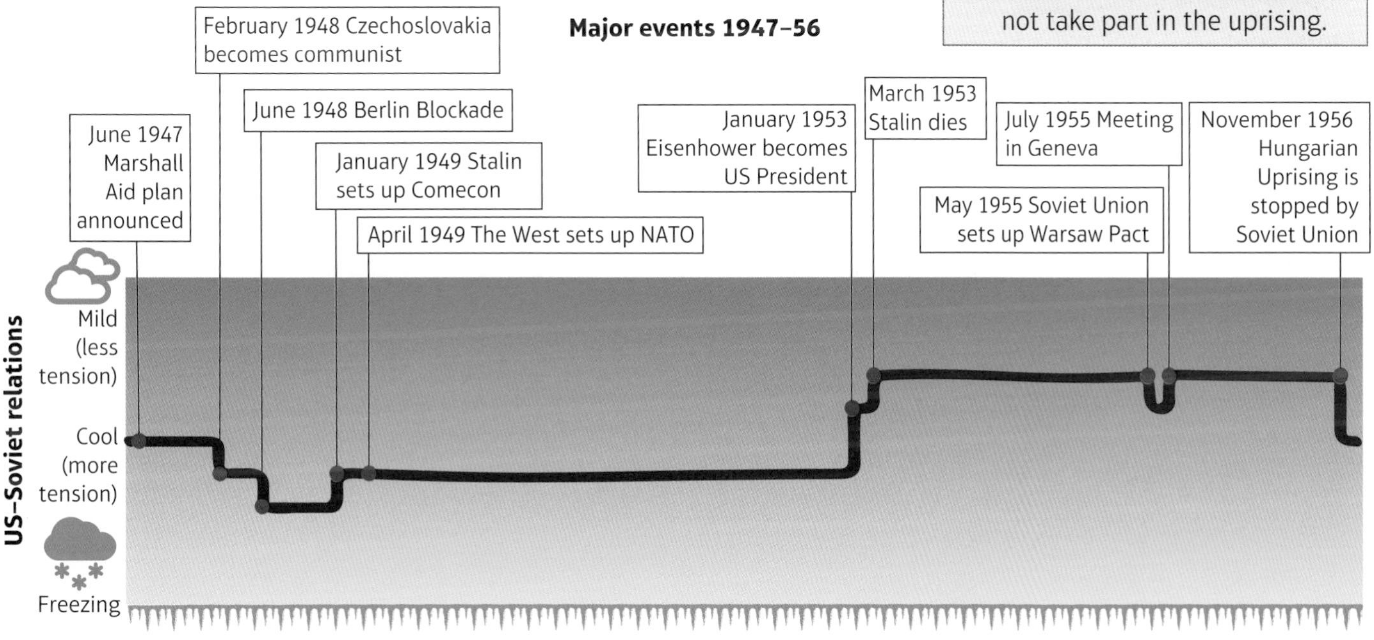

Major events 1947–56

February 1948 Czechoslovakia becomes communist

June 1948 Berlin Blockade

June 1947 Marshall Aid plan announced

January 1949 Stalin sets up Comecon

April 1949 The West sets up NATO

January 1953 Eisenhower becomes US President

March 1953 Stalin dies

July 1955 Meeting in Geneva

May 1955 Soviet Union sets up Warsaw Pact

November 1956 Hungarian Uprising is stopped by Soviet Union

US–Soviet relations

Mild (less tension)

Cool (more tension)

Freezing

Figure 1.9 The relationship between the USA and the Soviet Union, 1946–58.

Summary

- In the 1950s, there was an arms race between the USA and the Soviet Union. Both sides built up a stock of nuclear arms. They had enough weapons to destroy each other and the world several times over.
- In 1953, the election of Eisenhower and the death of Stalin seemed to lower tension in the Cold War.
- When West Germany joined NATO, the Soviets set up the Warsaw Pact.
- A rebellion against Soviet control of Hungary in 1956 was put down with armed force. The Hungarian Uprising seriously damaged East–West relations.

Checkpoint

Strengthen

S1 What new types of weapons were developed in the 1950s?

S2 What is meant by 'deterrent' in the Cold War?

S3 When did West Germany join NATO?

Challenge

C1 Why did Hungarians think their uprising would receive help from other countries?

How confident do you feel about your answers to these questions? If you're not sure you answered them well, form a group with other students, discuss the answers and then record your conclusions. Your teacher can give you some hints.

Recall quiz

1 Which countries were members of The Grand Alliance?
2 What years were the conferences at Tehran, Yalta and Potsdam held?
3 Who were the leaders of The Grand Alliance up to 1945? Who were the new leaders in that year?
4 What was the Truman Doctrine?
5 Explain what a 'satellite state' is.
6 Which countries joined NATO?
7 Which countries joined the Warsaw Pact?
8 In what year was West Germany created?
9 What is an ICBM?
10 Who was leader of the Soviet Union during the Hungarian Uprising?

Exam-style question, Section A

Explain **two** consequences of the Hungarian Uprising in 1956.   **8 marks**

Exam tip

Remember that 'consequences' are the outcomes or results. What happened because the Hungarian Uprising happened? For example, the Hungarian Uprising affected how many people viewed the Soviet Union.

You could start by writing 'One consequence of the Hungarian Uprising was…'

Activity

1 Copy the table below, but give it ten rows. Pick ten events between 1941 and 1958 and complete the columns to show their impact on relations between East and West. The first one is done for you.

Event	Brief summary	Did it improve or harm relations?
Formation of The Grand Alliance	The USA, the Soviet Union and Britain join to fight Hitler	Improved

2 Write a short paragraph explaining why Britain, the Soviet Union and the USA were allies until 1945. Why was the alliance difficult? Why did it end in 1945?
3 Give three reasons why Germany was divided into two parts.
4 Which of these statements do you agree with most?
   a Relations were better in 1945 than in 1958.
   b Relations were better in 1958 than 1945.
   c Relations were the same in 1945 and 1958.
With a partner discuss the reasons for your choice.

Writing historically: building information

When you are asked to write an explanation, you need to provide as much detailed information as possible. The best answers will link this detail to the main points.

Learning objectives

By the end of this lesson you will understand how to:

- add clear and detailed information to your writing
- use linking words to connect the detailed information to your main points.

Definitions

Detail: Detail in an exam answer means adding specific information. It could be dates, names, places, examples or facts.

Linking words: Words which can be used to link your points together.

How can I add detail to my writing?

Look at this exam-style question.

> Explain **two** consequences of the decisions made by The Grand Alliance at the Yalta Conference in February 1945. **(8 marks)**

Now look at one sentence from an answer to the question.

> The Grand Alliance agreed that Germany would be divided into four zones. These four zones were controlled by Britain, the USA, France and the Soviet Union.

The main point is highlighted in yellow. The extra detail has been highlighted in purple.

The extra detail develops the main point. It is not new information. It improves the point.

1. Why does the extra detail improve the point about the four zones?

2. What other details could have been added to improve the same point? Can you think of two other examples?

Using linking words can make answers shorter and clearer without losing any of the information. For example, the answer above has been rewritten into one sentence using a linking word.

> The Grand Alliance agreed that Germany would be divided into four zones, which were to be controlled by Britain, the USA, France and the Soviet Union.

The linking word is highlighted in green.

3. Why do you think the writer chose to use a linking word and write the answer in one sentence, instead of using two sentences?

Here are two easy linking words:

> who   which

You could also add a second word to the link, like this:

> which caused   which led to   who decided   which changed   which would   who thought

Now look at these four sentences taken from the same answer:

> *The Grand Alliance agreed that Germany would be divided into four zones. The zones were divided by checkpoints. The zones were supposed to be temporary. But the four zones ended up lasting a long time.*

4. How clear is the answer above?

5. Rewrite the answer, using linking words to make two sentences.

6. Which answer do you prefer: the four sentence example above or the two sentences you have written? Why?

Improving an answer

Look at this part of an answer to the same exam question on the previous page.

> *At the Yalta Conference the Grand Alliance agreed that Germany would pay reparations at the end of the war. This was to pay to repair damage to the other countries. They agreed that the total bill would be $20 billion. Half of this would go to the USSR. This was because they had suffered more damage than other countries.*

7. Rewrite this part of the answer using linking words to make it shorter and clearer.

8. Look carefully at what you wrote. Is it clear to read? Or is it a bit confusing? Does it have sentences that are too long? If so, try rewriting it to make it clearer.

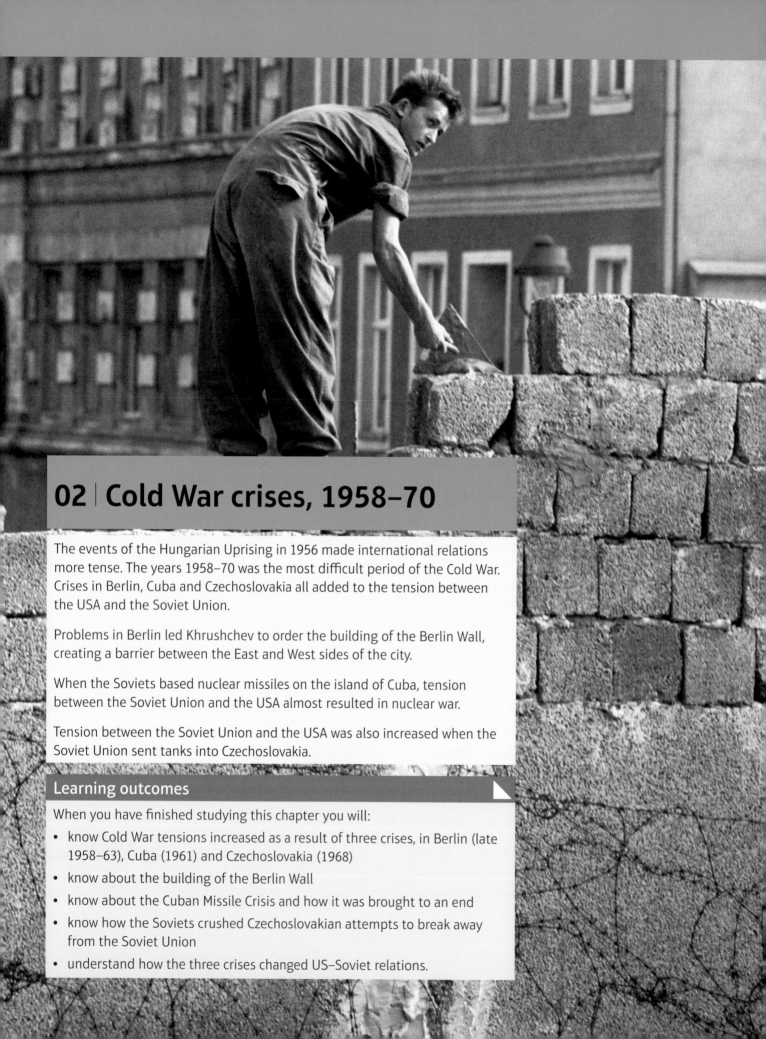

02 | Cold War crises, 1958–70

The events of the Hungarian Uprising in 1956 made international relations more tense. The years 1958–70 was the most difficult period of the Cold War. Crises in Berlin, Cuba and Czechoslovakia all added to the tension between the USA and the Soviet Union.

Problems in Berlin led Khrushchev to order the building of the Berlin Wall, creating a barrier between the East and West sides of the city.

When the Soviets based nuclear missiles on the island of Cuba, tension between the Soviet Union and the USA almost resulted in nuclear war.

Tension between the Soviet Union and the USA was also increased when the Soviet Union sent tanks into Czechoslovakia.

Learning outcomes

When you have finished studying this chapter you will:

- know Cold War tensions increased as a result of three crises, in Berlin (late 1958–63), Cuba (1961) and Czechoslovakia (1968)
- know about the building of the Berlin Wall
- know about the Cuban Missile Crisis and how it was brought to an end
- know how the Soviets crushed Czechoslovakian attempts to break away from the Soviet Union
- understand how the three crises changed US–Soviet relations.

Learning outcomes

- Understand why there was a crisis in Berlin, 1958–61.
- Know how Khrushchev tried to deal with the refugee problem and how Kennedy reacted.
- Understand how the Berlin Crisis affected international relations.

Timeline

Berlin Crisis, 1958–61

November 1958 Khrushchev's Berlin Ultimatum

September 1959 Khrushchev visits USA

September 1959 Camp David Summit meeting

June 1961 Vienna Summit meeting – Berlin Ultimatum renewed

June 1963 Kennedy visits Berlin

May 1959 Geneva Summit meeting

May 1960 U-2 Crisis

May 1960 Paris Summit meeting

August 1961 Construction of Berlin Wall begins

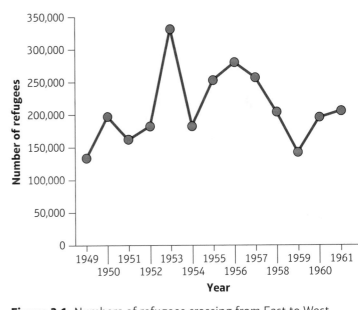

Figure 2.1 Numbers of refugees crossing from East to West Germany, 1949–61.

The refugee problem in Berlin, 1958

In 1949, Germany had been divided into West Germany and East Germany. West Germany was wealthier, due to Marshall Aid, whereas East Germany suffered from shortages of basic goods. There were also limits in East Germany on what people could say and do.

Three million East Germans chose to leave home and move to West Germany for a better life. All they had to do was travel from East to West Berlin. Once there, they could travel to West Germany.

By 1958, 3 million East Germans had fled to the West.

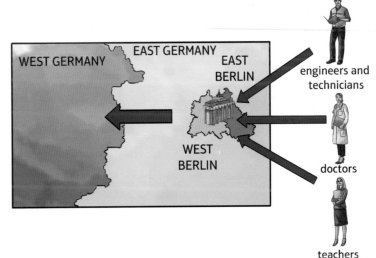

Figure: The brain drain. Many skilled workers left East Germany.

The Soviet leader, Khrushchev, could not allow this situation to continue. Not only was East Germany losing valuable people, but it made communism look bad because people were choosing the capitalist West.

Khrushchev's Berlin Ultimatum

Khrushchev decided the answer was for the whole of Berlin to become part of East Germany. If the Americans, British and French left Berlin, it would be much harder for East Germans to get into West Germany. On 27 November 1958, he issued the Berlin Ultimatum*.

Figure: Khrushchev's Berlin Ultimatum.

Key terms

Ultimatum*

A final demand, often backed up with a threat to take action.

Free city*

A city with its own independent government. Khrushchev did not really mean to make Berlin independent – he wanted it to be controlled by the Soviet Union.

Source A

Extract from Nikita Khrushchev's speech about Berlin, given on 10 November 1958.

The time has obviously arrived for the signatories of the Potsdam Agreement to renounce the remnants of the occupation regime in Berlin and thereby make it possible to create a normal situation in the capital of the German Democratic Republic. The Soviet Union, for its part, would hand over to the sovereign German Democratic Republic the functions in Berlin that are still exercised by Soviet agencies. This, I think, would be the correct thing to do.

Source B

This is an extract from a note sent from the Soviet Foreign Ministry to the US Ambassador at Moscow. It was titled 'Regarding Berlin' and sent on 27 November 1958. It became known as the Berlin Ultimatum.

If the statesmen responsible for the policy of the Western powers are guided by feelings of hatred for communism and the socialist countries in their approach to the Berlin question as well as other international problems, no good will come out of it.

The Berlin Ultimatum had a major impact on international relations. The West was annoyed by Khrushchev's demands and saw his actions as another example of the Soviet Union trying to spread communism. Khrushchev, however, saw his demands as essential to stop the flood of skilled workers from leaving East Germany.

By 1958, both the USA and the Soviet Union had large numbers of nuclear weapons and neither side wanted this crisis to lead to war. So between 1959 and 1961, talks were held to try to solve the 'Berlin problem'.

The summit meetings of 1959–61

Geneva, May 1959
Meeting 1

Both sides met and made suggestions as to how Berlin should be governed. They could not reach an agreement but at least they were able to discuss possibilities.

Camp David, September 1959
Meeting 2

Eisenhower and Khrushchev met face-to-face in the USA. There was no agreement, but the Soviets did withdraw the Berlin Ultimatum. The leaders appeared to get on better.

Paris, May 1960
Meeting 3

Just before the Paris meeting, the Soviet Union shot down an American U-2 spy-plane over Russia. The Americans said it was a weather plane but the pilot, Gary Powers, said that he was on a spying mission. Eisenhower refused to apologise. Khrushchev walked out of the meeting. No decisions were taken.

Source C

A photograph of Soviet people looking at the remains of the U-2 spy-plane shot down over the Soviet Union in May 1960.

Interpretation 1

A recent account of the Paris Summit meeting and U-2 incident from the *US Department of State Official History* website.

Khrushchev had publicly committed himself to the idea of 'peaceful coexistence*' with the United States... [Had] the United States apologized, he would have continued the summit. Eisenhower, however, refused to issue a formal apology... On May 11, Eisenhower finally acknowledged his full awareness of the entire program and of the Powers flight in particular. Moreover, he explained that... such spy flights were a necessary element in maintaining national defense, and that he planned to continue them.

Vienna, June 1961
Meeting 4

In January 1961, there was an election in the USA and Eisenhower lost. John F. Kennedy became the new president of the USA. Khrushchev believed that Kennedy was inexperienced, so it would be easy to get the better of him. He also knew that Kennedy had looked weak recently when a US invasion of Cuba at the 'Bay of Pigs' in 1961 failed (see page 50).

New talks were held in Vienna in June 1961. Khrushchev renewed the Berlin Ultimatum of 1958. Kennedy was determined not to appear weak and not to give away control of Berlin. He refused to accept the Ultimatum. They still couldn't reach a decision about Berlin.

After Vienna, Kennedy decided to increase spending on the US armed forces by over $2 billion. It looked like the USA was prepared to fight over Berlin.

Source D

President Kennedy speaking to the American people after his return from the Vienna Summit meeting in 1961.

We do not want to fight — but we have fought before. And others in earlier times have made the same dangerous mistake of assuming that the West was too selfish and too soft and too divided to resist invasions of freedom in other lands... We cannot and will not permit the Communists to drive us out of Berlin, either gradually or by force... Our pledge to that city is essential to the morale and security of Western Germany, to the unity of Western Europe, and to the faith of the entire Free World.

Activities

1   Write a sentence to summarise the results of each summit meeting held between 1959 and 1961.

2   For each summit meeting, list what went well and what went wrong. In a small group, discuss what made some summit meetings more successful than others and what would have made the talks more successful.

3   'The summit meetings were a complete waste of time.' How far do you agree with this statement? Write a short paragraph to explain your answer. You could start with 'I think that...'

Key term

Peaceful coexistence*

This means the two superpowers getting on without tension between them.

Building the Berlin Wall

As tension between East and West grew, more East Germans decided to cross to the West, just in case Khrushchev decided to close the border. On just one day in August 1961, for example, 40,000 East Germans crossed to the West.

On the night of 12 August 1961, East German troops built a barbed wire fence around Berlin and between East and West Berlin.

This was soon replaced with a concrete wall.

Impacts of the Berlin Wall

The impact in Berlin

The 3.6 metre high Berlin Wall cut through streets and even buildings. Between East and West Berlin there were two walls, one facing East, and the other West. They were separated by a zone known as 'no-man's land' packed with booby-traps, barbed wire, minefields with lookout towers, machine-gun nests and powerful searchlights. Families, were separated, often for years on end.

Figure: The Berlin Wall.

Source E

No-man's land between East and West Berlin.

In desperation, some people tried to cross the Wall. East German border guards were told to shoot anyone who tried and it is estimated that over 130 people were killed. One of the saddest failed attempts to cross the Berlin Wall came in August 1962, when two building workers made a dash for it. One reached West Berlin, but the other, Peter Fechter, was shot. He fell back into East Berlin and lay dying for 45 minutes. As thousands of West Germans yelled 'murderers' across the border, East German guards eventually took the body away.

Source F

The body of Peter Fechter is carried away by East German border guards after he was shot attempting to cross the Berlin Wall into West Berlin in 1962.

Activities ?

1   Look at Source E. Why do you think no one tried to rescue Peter Fechter?

2   In small groups, choose one of the following roles and prepare a 30-second speech to convince the rest of your class.

   a   President Kennedy saying why Khrushchev was wrong to build the Wall.

   b   Khrushchev explaining why he was right to build the Wall.

3   Which of these views do you think the people of Berlin would have agreed with? Give one reason for your choice.

Impact of the wall on the USA and the Soviet Union

The building of the Berlin Wall had positive and negative results for the USA and the Soviet Union.

	Negative outcomes	Positive outcomes
Soviet Union	Khrushchev had to abandon plans to control all of Germany. The Wall showed that the Soviet Union had to 'lock' people into East Germany to stop them leaving.	The Wall stopped refugees leaving for the West through East Berlin. The Wall sent the West a message that communism would survive in Berlin.
USA	The Soviet Union had built the wall without talking to the USA. Those people who wanted to escape from communism were no longer able to.	The Wall showed that Khrushchev had been forced to accept Western control in West Berlin. Khrushchev learned that he could not bully Kennedy.

The positive results for Kennedy's reputation were demonstrated when he visited West Berlin in 1963. Thousands of West Berliners turned out to see him. He was treated like a rock star or sporting hero – his route was showered with flowers, rice and shredded paper and crowds chanted his name.

During the visit, Kennedy praised the freedoms of the West and compared them with communism in a famous speech in which he said, 'Ich bin ein Berliner.' ('I am a citizen of Berlin.')

Source H

John F. Kennedy giving the 'Ich bin ein Berliner' speech, on 26 June 1963.

Source G

From a speech given by Kennedy on 26 June 1963. The speech was given in a public square in Berlin.

Two thousand years ago the proudest boast was 'civis Romanus sum' [I am a Roman citizen]. Today, in the world of freedom, the proudest boast is 'Ich bin ein Berliner' [I am a citizen of Berlin].

There are many people in the world who really don't understand, or say they don't, what is the great issue between the free world and the communist world. Let them come to Berlin.

There are some who say that communism is the future. Let them come to Berlin.

And there are some who say in Europe and elsewhere we can work with the Communists. Let them come to Berlin.

And there are even a few who say that it is true that Communism is an evil system, but it permits us to make economic progress. Lass' sie nach Berlin kommen. Let them come to Berlin.

Extend your knowledge

'Ich bin ein Berliner'

In Kennedy's 1963 speech in Berlin, he said 'Ich bin ein Berliner'. 'Berliner' means 'citizen of Berlin' but also 'doughnut' – so some people have argued that Kennedy literally said 'I am a doughnut'! The crowd in Berlin doesn't seem to have thought this, or cared if that was what he said. They loved Kennedy's message and the fact that he tried to say it in German.

Impacts on international relations

Although the building of the Wall led to increased tension between the Soviet Union and the USA, there were also positive results.

Negative outcomes	Positive outcomes
The two sides had been arguing about Germany since the Second World War. Now things were so bad that the Soviets had built a concrete wall dividing Germany.	Now Berlin was divided and the borders between East and West Germany were closed, it was less likely that the US and the Soviet Union would go to war over Berlin. Kennedy said, a wall was better than war.
The Berlin Wall became a powerful symbol of the differences between East and West for almost 30 years, until it was taken down in 1989.	So, in some ways, the Wall may have reduced tension between the USA and the Soviet Union.

However, any improvement in relations was soon destroyed by events in Cuba in 1962.

Exam-style question, Section A

Write a narrative account analysing the key events of the 'Berlin Crisis' in the years 1958–61.

You may use the following in your answer:

- the Berlin Ultimatum, 1958
- the construction of the Berlin Wall.

You **must** also use information of your own. **8 marks**

Exam tip

The key to this question is to link the events together.

The best answers use linking phrases, like 'as a result', 'this led to' or 'this caused'. You can find other ideas on page 91.

Summary

- Khrushchev was worried about East German citizens crossing into West Germany.
- Talks between the USA and the Soviet Union about Berlin broke down.
- Khrushchev decided to build the Berlin Wall.
- Kennedy visited West Berlin to show his support.
- The Berlin Wall now acted as a symbol of the division of Europe.

Checkpoint

Strengthen

S1 What was Khrushchev's Berlin Ultimatum?

S2 Why did he issue this ultimatum?

S3 Why did the Paris Summit meeting in 1960 fail?

Challenge

C1 In what way could the building of the Berlin Wall have helped relations between the USA and the Soviet Union?

How confident do you feel about your answers to these questions? Form a small group and discuss any questions you are not sure about. Look for the answers in this section. Now rewrite your answers together in your group.

Learning outcomes

- Understand why Cuba became a threat to the USA.
- Know how Kennedy dealt with Khrushchev's attempt to put nuclear missiles on Cuba.
- Understand how the crisis affected international relations.

The Cuban Revolution

In January 1959, a group of revolutionaries replaced President Batista and the pro-American government of Cuba. President Eisenhower was concerned about the revolution*. American businesses had invested a lot of money in Cuba. In particular, the USA bought a lot of Cuba's sugar. The new leader of Cuba, Fidel Castro, did not want his country's economy to be under US control. This created tension between the USA and Cuba.

There were three main areas of tension:

- The US government refused to help Cuba economically, unless Cuba followed the same economic rules as the USA.
- In May 1959, the Cuban government took over all land in Cuba owned by foreigners. Many were Americans.
- Castro appointed Communists to his government. Then, in February 1960, he made an agreement with the Soviet Union for it to buy Cuban sugar. In return, Cuba would receive weapons from the Soviet Union.

Key term

Revolution*

This is where people take over a government and replace it with a new leader.

Timeline

Cuban Revolution and the Cuban Missile Crisis, 1959–63

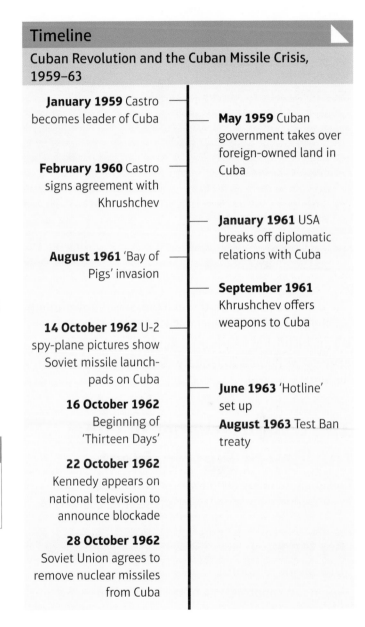

January 1959 Castro becomes leader of Cuba

May 1959 Cuban government takes over foreign-owned land in Cuba

February 1960 Castro signs agreement with Khrushchev

January 1961 USA breaks off diplomatic relations with Cuba

August 1961 'Bay of Pigs' invasion

September 1961 Khrushchev offers weapons to Cuba

14 October 1962 U-2 spy-plane pictures show Soviet missile launch-pads on Cuba

16 October 1962 Beginning of 'Thirteen Days'

June 1963 'Hotline' set up

August 1963 Test Ban treaty

22 October 1962 Kennedy appears on national television to announce blockade

28 October 1962 Soviet Union agrees to remove nuclear missiles from Cuba

Fidel Castro and Nikita Khrushchev meet at the United Nations in New York, in 1960.

The USA was very worried that a pro-Soviet government was being established just 145 kilometres from the US mainland. In 1960, President Eisenhower banned all trade with Cuba. In January 1961, the USA broke off diplomatic relations* with Cuba.

The USA intervenes in Cuba: the 'Bay of Pigs' incident

President Kennedy (who took over from Eisenhower in 1961) did not want a Soviet ally so close to the USA.

Key terms

Diplomatic relations*

When two countries talk to sort out any problems and work together.

CIA*

The Central Intelligence Agency. Part of the US government that is responsible for spying and security.

Cuban exiles*

People from Cuba who had left because of the revolution but wanted to go back and defeat the new government.

The CIA* suggested that a group of Cuban exiles* could be trained to launch an invasion and overthrow Castro.

On 17 April 1961, an invasion force of around 1,400 Cuban exiles landed at the 'Bay of Pigs' in Cuba.

The USA hoped they would overthrow the Castro regime and put a new US-friendly government in control of the island. This was a complete failure.

Figure: Reasons for failure of Bay of Pigs invasion.

Castro showed wrecked aeroplanes and other evidence of the Cuban victory to journalists from around the world. The defeat embarrassed the USA.

Source B

Anti-Castro fighters captured during the 'Bay of Pigs' operation.

Effects of the 'Bay of Pigs' incident on international relations

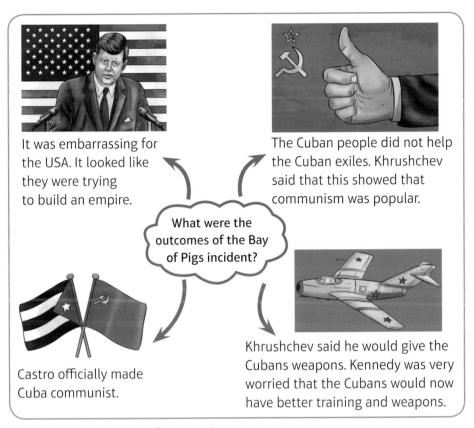

Figure: Impact of the Bay of Pigs incident.

Cuba is very near to the USA, so the USA became worried that Cuba could be used as a base for the USSR to threaten them.

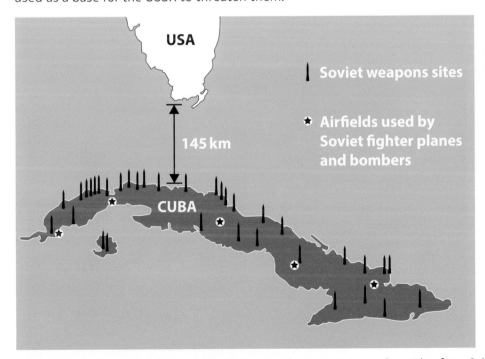

Figure 2.2 Soviet missile bases and airfields on Cuba in 1962. It is only 145 km from Cuba to the USA.

Source C

Extracts from a 1961 US government inquiry into the 'Bay of Pigs' operation.

Scrutiny* of the plans for the operation would have shown that Castro's ability to fight back and roll up internal opposition needed to be taken more seriously... Why did the United States contemplate* pitting 1,500 soldiers, however well-trained and armed, against an enemy vastly superior in number and arms. We can confidently assert* that the CIA had no evidence that Cubans in significant numbers would join the invaders... The project has lost all elements of secrecy as for more than three months the American press had been reporting on the recruitment and training of Cubans. The CIA's name was freely linked with these activities. Denial was a pathetic illusion.

Key terms

Scrutiny*
To look very closely at something.

Contemplate*
To think about something.

Assert*
To make a claim.

Activities ?

1 Why was the USA worried about Castro's takeover in Cuba?

2 Explain what the USA wanted to happen from the 'Bay of Pigs' invasion.

3 Source C says, 'Denial was a pathetic illusion'. This is an excellent 'soundbite'. Work with a partner:

 a What does this source mean? Use as few words as possible.

 b What does the report say went wrong with the invasion?

Key term

Intelligence agencies*

Parts of the government which spy and investigate, and advise the leader of what to do.

NATO* (North Atlantic Treaty Organisaton)

A military alliance between the USA and Western European countries, created in 1949.

The Cuban Missile Crisis

On 14 October 1962, an American U-2 spy-plane took pictures of launch-pads on Cuba for ballistic missiles, which could carry nuclear warheads. US intelligence agencies* told President Kennedy that a fleet of Soviet ships was sailing to Cuba, which were likely to be carrying the missiles.

NATO* had missiles in Turkey, near the Soviet Union. Khrushchev wanted them removed.

 Khrushchev had looked weak over Berlin. He wanted to look strong.

Khrushchev wanted to protect communism in Cuba.

Figure: Why Khrushchev tried to put missiles on Cuba.

Source D

This photo, taken on 23 October 1962 by an American U-2 spy-plane, showed that further work had been done on the missile launch site in Cuba since it was originally spotted on 14 October.

Why did Cuba matter? The Soviet Union could fire nuclear missiles from Russia. They did not need Cuba. But it was important politically because it made the USA look weak. Kennedy had to take action. But his advisers said he only had two weeks until the missiles could be ready.

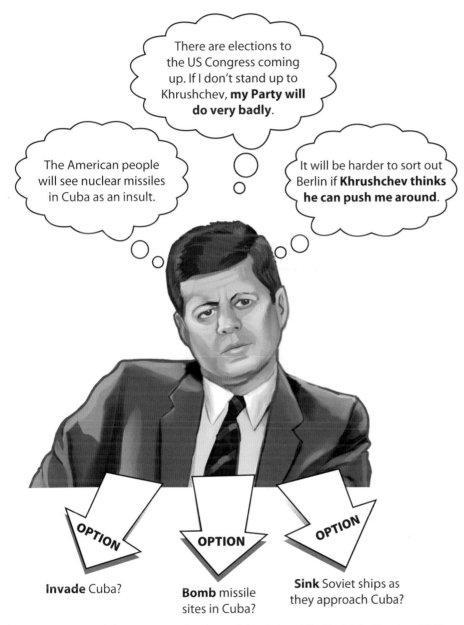

Figure 2.3 Kennedy's options at the time of the Cuban Missile Crisis, October 1962.

Source E

An extract from a statement made by Dean Acheson, one of Kennedy's advisers, at a meeting held on 17 October 1962 to discuss what action the USA should take over Cuba.

We should proceed at once with the necessary military action and do no talking. The Soviets will react someplace. We must expect this, take the consequences and manage the situations as they evolve. We should have no consultations* with Khrushchev, Castro or our allies, though we should alert our allies.

Key term

Consultations*
To talk about something with another person to hear their opinion.

Activities ?

1 Khrushchev must have known that the USA would object to Soviet nuclear missiles being placed in Cuba. What are two reasons why he would still try to do so?

2 Look at Source E.

   a Summarise Acheson's point-of-view in one sentence.

   b Was Acheson a Hawk or a Dove*?

   c Does Source E prove that the USA was prepared to fight the Soviet Union?

Key terms

Hawks and Doves*

Advisers who supported war were known as Hawks. Those who wanted to avoid war were known as Doves.

Blockade*

When a military force refuses to let something past or they will open fire.

Confrontation*

When two countries challenge each other and there is a risk of war.

The Thirteen Days

16 October – Kennedy called his advisers together to decide what to do about the Soviet ships. His 'Hawks*' advised him to be aggressive.

22 October – Kennedy decided to set up a blockade* around Cuba. He announced it on television and got the US military ready for war, including fighter planes with nuclear warheads.

24 October – Soviet ships reached the US blockade and turned around.

From confrontation* to agreement

26 October – Khrushchev sent a telegram to Kennedy offering to remove missiles from Cuba if the USA agreed not to invade the island.

27 October – Khrushchev sent another telegram, demanding that the USA remove their missiles from Turkey. Kennedy agreed publicly not to invade Cuba, and privately to remove the missiles in Turkey.

28 October – Khrushchev agreed to remove missiles from Cuba.

The consequences of the Cuban Missile Crisis

The Cuban Missile Crisis made clear what could happen if the Soviet Union or the USA continued to follow a policy of brinkmanship*. Both countries now wanted to make sure that future misunderstandings would not cause war to break out. Four important steps were taken.

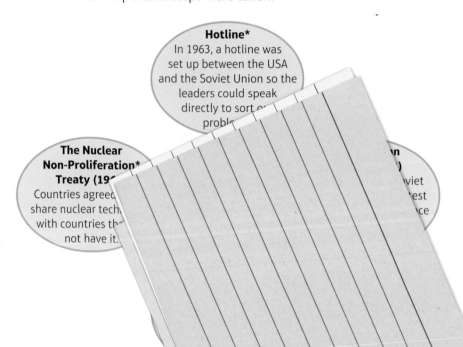

Hotline*
In 1963, a hotline was set up between the USA and the Soviet Union so the leaders could speak directly to sort out problems.

The Nuclear Non-Proliferation* Treaty (19...)
Countries agreed ... share nuclear tech... with countries th... not have it.

Figure: Outcomes of the Cuban ...

In some ways the Cuban Missile ... safer place:

- The USA and the Soviet Union h... of nuclear war.

- Kennedy and Khrushchev's relation...

Kennedy had shown himself to be a str... Soviet Union. This made him more popul... people did not find out that the US missile...

But Khrushchev looked weak even though he ... urce F). He was so unpopular in the Soviet Union that ... as leader in 1964.

Source F

An extract from Khrushchev's memoirs, published in 1967.

We sent the Americans a note saying that we agreed to remove our missiles and bombers on condition that President Kennedy gave us assurances that there would be no invasion of Cuba. Finally Kennedy gave in and agreed to make a statement giving us such an assurance. It was a great victory for us — a spectacular success without having to fire a single shot.

Key terms

Brinkmanship*
Pushing disagreements to the point where there is a risk of war.

Hotline*
A direct communication line between the leaders of the USA and the Soviet Union.

Non-proliferation*
Stopping the spread of something, usually weapons or armaments.

Source G

A cartoon published in the Washington Post on 1 November 1962.

A 1962 Herblock Cartoon, © The Herb Block Foundation.

Extend your knowledge

Deadly nuclear power

Researchers at Harvard University worked out that if the USA and the Soviet Union had fired nuclear missiles at each other during the Cuban Missile Crisis, about 100 million people would have died in each country.

Activities ?

1   Do you think that Kennedy or Khrushchev won the Cuban Missile Crisis? Give one reason for your answer.

2   Read Source F.

  a) What is Khrushchev trying to claim?

  b) Are you surprised that Khrushchev was sacked in 1964?

3   Look at Source G.

  a) In your own words describe the cartoonist's view of the Cuban Missile Crisis.

  b) Do you agree with the cartoonist?

Exam-style question ●

Explain the importance of the 'Bay of Pigs' invasion for relations between the USA and the Soviet Union.   **8 marks**

Exam tip ●

Note the question asks about importance and also gives you a focus for that importance – relations between the USA and the Soviet Union. Don't just say what happened. Explain how the invasion affected relations. Did it make them better or worse?

You could start your first point by writing 'The "Bay of Pigs" invasion was important for relations between the USA and the Soviet Union because…'

You could think about how it made the USA look, and how that changed their relationship with the Soviet Union.

Summary

- The pro-American government in Cuba was overthrown.
- The USA supported Cuban exiles trying to put back a pro-American government.
- Castro turned to the Soviet Union for support.
- Khrushchev decided to place nuclear missiles in Cuba.
- Kennedy set up a naval blockade. This led to a crisis known as the 'Thirteen Days'.

Checkpoint

Strengthen

S1 What actions did Castro take which worried the USA?

S2 Briefly summarise the events of the 'Thirteen Days'.

S3 What positive things happened as a result of the Cuban Missile Crisis?

Challenge

C1 Why didn't the USA attack the Soviet ships bringing missiles to Cuba?

How confident do you feel about your answers to these questions? Re-read the section and then try answering the questions again. If you're still not sure, discuss with your teacher.

Timeline

The 'Prague Spring' and its impact, 1968–69

January 1968 Dubcek becomes leader of Czech government

April 1968 'Prague Spring' begins

August 1968 Soviet invasion of Czechoslovakia

September 1968 The Brezhnev Doctrine

April 1969 Dubcek sacked

Key terms

Satellite state*

Countries in Eastern Europe which became communist after the Second World War.

Consumer goods*

Goods bought by people for their personal use.

Censored*

When a government stops people writing or saying things it does not like.

Socialism*

Communist countries sometimes refer to themselves as 'socialist'.

Reforms*

When a government passes laws to make changes.

Opposition to Soviet control

In 1948, Czechoslovakia had become a communist satellite state*.

Life under communist rule was difficult for the Czech people. In effect, the country was ruled by the Soviet Union, which used the secret police to maintain control. The economy was poor. There were few consumer goods*. There was no freedom of speech and radio, newspapers and television were censored*. The government arrested many politicians and citizens.

In 1966, students started to protest against the unpopular government.

The 'Prague Spring'

In 1968, Alexander Dubcek became the head of the Czech government. The Soviet leadership trusted Dubcek to make the government of Czechoslovakia less unpopular, while staying loyal to the Soviet Union. Dubcek believed that communism was good but should not make life miserable for people. He called this 'socialism* with a human face'.

The reforms* Dubcek introduced from April 1968 became known as the 'Prague Spring'.

Figure: Dubcek's 'Prague Spring' reforms.

Dubcek's reforms were very popular with the Czech people, but they were much less popular in Moscow. Dubcek promised Moscow that Czechoslovakia would stay in the Warsaw Pact*.

However, the Soviet leader, Brezhnev (who replaced Khrushchev in 1968), was worried. What if other Warsaw Pact countries wanted similar reforms? He was already worried about the loyalty of Romania and Yugoslavia. What if Moscow also lost control of Czechoslovakia?

Key term

Warsaw Pact*

The military alliance of the Soviet Union and the communist satellite states.

Figure 2.4 The Warsaw Pact troops that helped put down the 'Prague Spring' came from East Germany, Hungary and the Soviet Union.

Source A

Czech citizens inspect a captured Soviet tank in Prague in August 1968.

The Soviet reaction

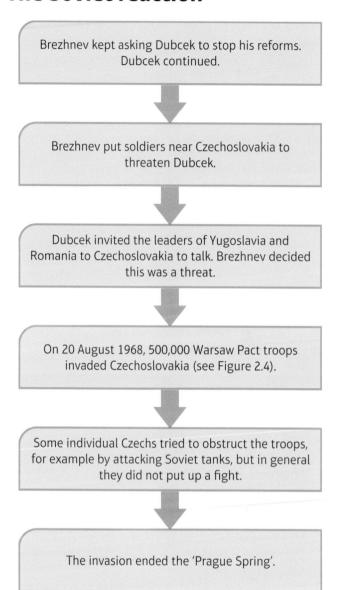

Brezhnev kept asking Dubcek to stop his reforms. Dubcek continued.

Brezhnev put soldiers near Czechoslovakia to threaten Dubcek.

Dubcek invited the leaders of Yugoslavia and Romania to Czechoslovakia to talk. Brezhnev decided this was a threat.

On 20 August 1968, 500,000 Warsaw Pact troops invaded Czechoslovakia (see Figure 2.4).

Some individual Czechs tried to obstruct the troops, for example by attacking Soviet tanks, but in general they did not put up a fight.

The invasion ended the 'Prague Spring'.

Figure: The Prague Spring.

Source B

A young journalist describes the moment when the Soviet troops arrived.

```
I remember very well the face of the first
Soviet soldier I saw. He was carrying a huge
machine gun, and looked like he'd just stepped
out of a film about the battle of Stalingrad.
He was very dirty, and his face was full of
sweat. It was absolutely ridiculous, absolutely
absurd. I tried to talk to him, but it was
pointless, he wouldn't speak to me. Even later
on, when I did manage to speak to some of the
soldiers, it was useless. They were totally
indoctrinated. They believed they had prevented
the outbreak of World War III or something.
```

Dubcek was arrested, sent to Moscow and ordered to end his reforms. Then in 1969 he was replaced as leader. The new leader was a hardline communist* who arrested over a thousand Czechs. The Soviet Union was back in control in Czechoslovakia.

Activities ?

1 In a small group, list as many reasons as you can why communism was unpopular in Czechoslovakia before 1968.

2 Look at the list of reforms Dubcek put forward in the 'Prague Spring'. Explain how each one might make communism more popular.

3 Can you think of any reason why Brezhnev sent Dubcek back to Prague in 1968, instead of sacking him straight away?

Key terms

Hardline communist*

Someone who is a strong supporter of communism.

Doctrine*

A belief or philosophy.

Shirking*

Not doing something which is a responsibility.

International obligations*

A country's responsibilities to other countries that are their allies.

The Brezhnev Doctrine

To the West, Brezhnev's actions appeared to be another example of the Soviet Union controlling another European country.

But Brezhnev said that it was necessary to protect all communist countries. He said that if a country did something which threatened communism, all other communist countries would take action to stop them. This was known as the Brezhnev Doctrine*.

One communist country's actions affect all other communist countries. If a communist country threatens the future of communism, we will all take action.

This will stop other countries copying Czechoslovakia and making reforms.

Figure: The meaning behind the Brezhnev Doctrine.

Source C

The Brezhnev Doctrine, as explained in the Soviet newspaper *Pravda* in September 1968.

```
Every communist party is responsible not only
to its own people, but also to... the entire
communist movement. Whoever forgets this is
placing sole emphasis on the independence of
their own communist party and shirking* their
international obligations*.
```

The impact of the 'Prague Spring' and the Soviet invasion

What happened in Czechoslovakia	The invasion ended the 'Prague Spring'. The government soon put things back to the way they had been.
What happened to the relations between the communist countries	• The Communist governments of Yugoslavia and Romania condemned the Soviet invasion. • Some Communist Parties cut links to the Soviet Union. But Poland and East Germany were pleased. They felt safe from people who wanted reform. • Warsaw Pact countries were less likely to make reforms as they remembered what happened in Czechoslovakia.
What happened to the relations between the USA and the Soviet Union	• The USA and other Western governments protested to the Soviet Union. • Some countries in the United Nations criticised the invasion, but no action was taken. • No Western countries sent troops, so Brezhnev looked strong. He realised that countries would complain but take no action.
What happened to the USA's international reputation	The USA was fighting in the Vietnam War. It did not want to get involved in Czechoslovakia. Other countries saw that the USA criticised but did not do anything.

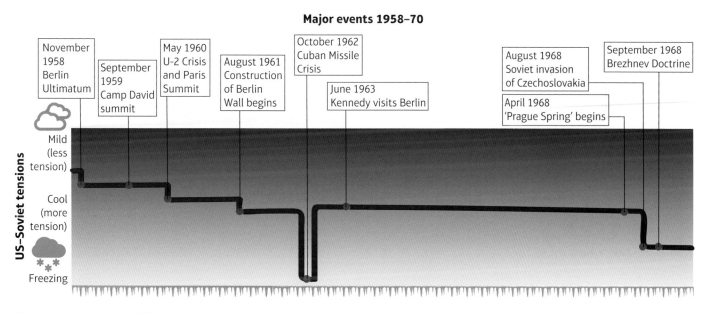

Figure 2.5 Rising and falling tensions between the USA and Soviet Union, 1958–70.

Exam-style question

Explain **two** consequences of the election of Alexander Dubcek as First Secretary of the Czech Communist Party in January 1968. **8 marks**

Exam tip

This question asks about 'consequences' so think about what difference the election of Dubcek made. How did his election change things? You need to make sure that the two consequences are different to each other. For example, if the first consequence is about the reforms that Dubcek made, the second consequence needs to be something different, such as how the relationship between Czechoslovakia and the Soviet Union changed.

Summary

- Communist rule in Czechoslovakia became more unpopular.
- Dubcek introduced reforms in the 'Prague Spring'.
- Brezhnev told Dubcek not to go too far with his reforms.
- When Dubcek did not stop his reforms, Brezhnev ordered tanks into Czechoslovakia.
- The Brezhnev Doctrine was issued.

Checkpoint

Strengthen

S1 How did Dubcek's reforms change Czechoslovakia?

S2 Why did Brezhnev disapprove of the reforms?

S3 Why do you think the reforms are known as the 'Prague Spring'?

Challenge

C1 Do you think the events of the 'Prague Spring' increased or reduced support for communism in Europe?

How confident do you feel about your answers to these questions? Discuss any you are unsure about with a partner then try rewriting your answers together.

Recap: Cold War crises, 1958–70

Recall quiz

1. Why was Berlin divided?
2. Why was the Soviet Union worried about Berlin in the years 1958–61?
3. Who were the presidents of the USA from 1958 to 1970?
4. Who were the leaders of the Soviet Union from 1958 to 1970?
5. Why did Kennedy visit Berlin in 1963?
6. When did Fidel Castro gain power in Cuba?
7. What was the 'Bay of Pigs' incident?
8. What three agreements were made as a result of the Cuban crisis?
9. What was the 'Prague Spring'?
10. What actions did Brezhnev take to end the 'Prague Spring'?

Activities

1. Write two reasons to explain why events in Berlin in 1958 almost led to war.
2. Write two reasons to explain why events in Cuba in 1962 almost led to war.
3. Why would the Soviet Union not accept 'socialism with a human face' in Czechoslovakia? Write your answer in a short paragraph.

Exam-style question, Section A

Explain **two** of the following:

- the importance of Kennedy's 1963 speech for the future of Germany
- the importance of the 'Bay of Pigs' incident for the future of Cuba
- the importance of the 'Prague Spring' for relations between the USA and the Soviet Union.

16 marks

Exam tip

Remember that this question is not asking for a description of an event or policy. It is asking about why that event or policy was important. What difference did it make?

Read the question carefully. For example, the 'Prague Spring' affected the Czech people's lives, but the last question is asking how it changed relations between the USA and the Soviet Union.

Writing historically: linking information

When you explain events and their consequences, you need to show how your ideas link together. We already saw some ways to link ideas on pages 38–39.

Learning outcomes

By the end of this lesson, you will understand how to:

- link two points together using linking words.

Definitions

Linking words: Words which can be used to link two or more points together.

Verb: An action word, such as 'announce' or 'invade'.

How can I link my ideas?

Look at this exam-style question.

> Explain **two** consequences of the election of Alexander Dubcek as First Secretary of the Czech Communist Party in 1968. **(8 marks)**

Now look at how these two sentences which answer the question can be linked together.

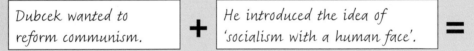

| Dubcek wanted to reform communism. | **+** | He introduced the idea of 'socialism with a human face'. | **=** |

> Dubcek wanted to reform communism, so he introduced the idea of 'socialism with a human face'.

Even though this answer only added the linking word 'so', it shows that the two ideas are connected. This improves the quality of the explanation in the answer.

1. Look at the sentences below. How could you link them using a connecting word?

| Communist rule in Czechoslovakia became more unpopular. | **+** | There were mass protests on the streets of Prague. | **=** |
| Brezhnev wanted to re-establish Soviet control over Czechoslovakia. | **+** | He ordered Warsaw Pact troops to march on Prague. | **=** |

2. Choose one of the sentences above. Can you think of one or two more ways of linking them?

3. Which of your new sentences do you like the most? Why?

Improving sentences

On pages 38, 39 and 64, we looked at adding detail and links to sentences. Let's see if we can improve some of these sentences using what we have learned. Look at this question:

> Explain **two** of the following:
> - The importance of the 'Bay of Pigs' incident for international relations.
> - The importance of the Cuban Missile Crisis for Kennedy's reputation.
> - The importance of the Soviet invasion of Czechoslovakia, 1963, for Brezhnev's reputation. **(16 marks)**

Look at this part of an answer to the first option:

> The Bay of Pigs made the USA look like a weak country. The Cuban exiles they had sent were captured.

We could improve this as:

> The Bay of Pigs made the USA look like a weak country due to the capture of the Cuban exiles that they had sent.

The detail has been linked so that it supports the first idea. In this example, some of the words have changed order to use a different linking word to 'because'.

4. For each of the sentences below, add a detail which supports the idea and link it together with a connecting word. There are some ideas for connecting words in the box at the bottom.

> The USA looked like an aggressive country trying to build an empire.

> Kennedy looked like a foolish and inexperienced leader.

> The Soviet Union and Cuba looked stronger.

What connecting words can I use?

There are lots of connecting words. If you need ideas, how about these:
- as a result
- which meant that
- because
- due to
- since
- on the grounds that

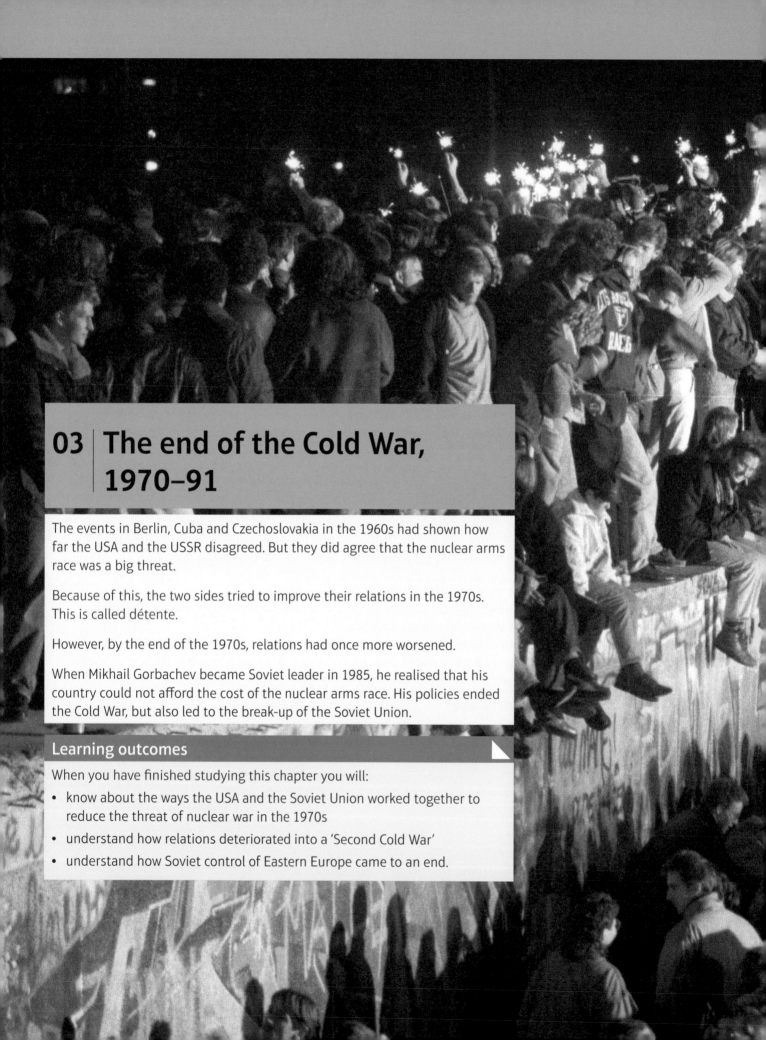

03 | The end of the Cold War, 1970–91

The events in Berlin, Cuba and Czechoslovakia in the 1960s had shown how far the USA and the USSR disagreed. But they did agree that the nuclear arms race was a big threat.

Because of this, the two sides tried to improve their relations in the 1970s. This is called détente.

However, by the end of the 1970s, relations had once more worsened.

When Mikhail Gorbachev became Soviet leader in 1985, he realised that his country could not afford the cost of the nuclear arms race. His policies ended the Cold War, but also led to the break-up of the Soviet Union.

Learning outcomes

When you have finished studying this chapter you will:
- know about the ways the USA and the Soviet Union worked together to reduce the threat of nuclear war in the 1970s
- understand how relations deteriorated into a 'Second Cold War'
- understand how Soviet control of Eastern Europe came to an end.

3.1 Attempts to reduce tension between East and West, 1969–79

Timeline

Détente, 1969–79

1968 Nixon elected President of the USA

1972 SALT 1

1973 The Soviet leader Brezhnev visits Washington

1975 Helsinki Accords, Apollo-Soyuz space mission

1979 SALT 2

Key terms

Détente*

A period of peace between two groups that were previously at war, or hostile to each other.

Domestic*

Things that happen inside a country.

Anti-war demonstrations*

Protests in USA against the Vietnam War and nuclear warfare.

But the Cuban Missile Crisis (see page 49) showed that even if no one wanted a war, one could still happen by accident if either side lost control.

Because of this, during the 1970s, the USA and the Soviet Union tried to co-operate. This is known as détente*.

Détente

After the Second World War, an arms race developed between the USA and the Soviet Union. This included making nuclear warheads carried on long distance missiles. Both sides had enough to totally destroy each other. This was called 'Mutually Assured Destruction', or MAD. Because of this the USA and the Soviet Union wanted to avoid war.

Why did the USA and the Soviet Union follow a policy of détente at this time?

Both the USA and the USSR saw détente as a way of avoiding nuclear war. It was also a good way of saving money.

However, each side also had their own domestic* reasons for following détente:

The USA was busy with the Vietnam War which was expensive.

There were lots of anti-war demonstrations* in the USA.

Why did the USA want to follow détente?

There were protests in the USA about the treatment of black people and tensions between rich and poor. When civil rights campaigner Martin Luther King was murdered in 1968, there were massive riots.

Richard Nixon was elected president of the USA in 1968. He had different priorities than the presidents before him, wanting to focus on the USA's social problems and the Vietnam War.

Figure: Reasons why the USA wanted détente.

Source A

The effects of rioting on the streets of Chicago, in April 1968, following the assassination of Martin Luther King.

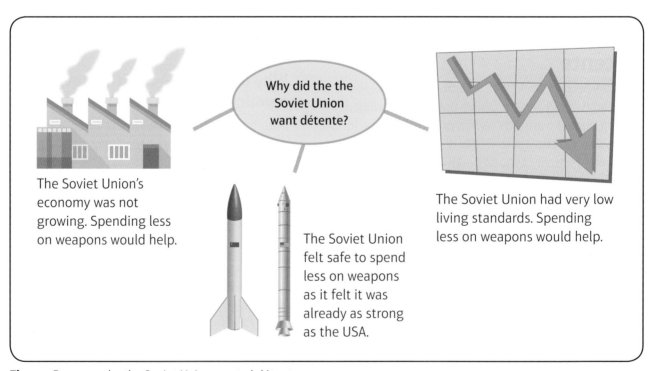

The Soviet Union's economy was not growing. Spending less on weapons would help.

Why did the the Soviet Union want détente?

The Soviet Union felt safe to spend less on weapons as it felt it was already as strong as the USA.

The Soviet Union had very low living standards. Spending less on weapons would help.

Figure: Reasons why the Soviet Union wanted détente.

Both sides saw détente as a way of saving money and being able to focus on problems in their own country.

Things also started to improve in Europe. From 1969, relations between East and West Germany improved (though the Berlin Wall was still there). Other Eastern and Western countries started to get on better as well.

SALT 1

In 1972, the USA and the Soviet Union signed an agreement which would limit the number of nuclear weapons each side had.

SALT (Strategic Arms Limitation Treaty) 1			
What did they agree?	What were the strengths of the treaty?	What were the weaknesses of the treaty?	What were the consequences of the treaty?
• Each side could only have 740 SLBMs*. • The USA could have 1,054 ICBMs* and the Soviet Union could have 1,618. The Soviet Union was allowed more as the USA had more bomber planes. • Each side could only have 200 ABMs* for shooting down ICBMs. • They agreed to try to avoid nuclear war.	• The treaty showed that both sides were willing to discuss limiting nuclear weapons. • Both sides wanted to reach an agreement and avoid future war.	• The plan assumed that if a war started both sides would follow the agreement just because they had signed a piece of paper. • Both sides still had more than enough nuclear weapons to destroy each other. • The treaty did not cover all types of weapon, like the new MIRVs*.	• In 1972, after the treaty, President Nixon visited Soviet leader Brezhnev. In 1973, Brezhnev visited Nixon in the USA. This improved their relationship. • In 1974, they started new SALT 2 talks to improve the SALT 1 agreement.

Key terms

SLBM*

A submarine launched ballistic missile. A missile fired from a submarine with a nuclear warhead.

ICBM*

Intercontinental ballistic missile. A long range missile which can travel more than 5,500 km and carry a nuclear warhead.

ABM*

Anti-ballistic missile. A missile that could shoot down ICBMs.

MIRV*

Multiple independently targeted re-entry vehicle. A new type of missile which carried several nuclear warheads on one weapon.

Activities ?

1   Write a paragraph to explain why the USA and the Soviet Union decided to follow a policy of détente in the 1970s. You should mention at least one reason for each side.

2   Read the two statements and decide which one you agree with more. What are two reasons that support that statement?

   a   'SALT 1 was a valuable move towards world peace.'

   b   'SALT 1 had too many weaknesses to be considered a valuable agreement.'

Key terms

White House*

The building that the President of the USA lives and works in.

NATO* (North Atlantic Treaty Organisaton)

A military alliance between the USA and Western European countries, created in 1949.

Warsaw Pact*

The military alliance of the Soviet Union and the communist satellite states.

Accord*

Another word for a treaty, something that is agreed between countries.

Human rights*

Basic human freedoms, like the freedom to say what you think or to follow your chosen religion.

Source B

President Nixon with the Soviet leader, Brezhnev during their meeting at the White House* in 1973.

The Helsinki Accords, 1975

In 1973, 35 nations from NATO* and the Warsaw Pact* met to agree a treaty to improve relations. In August 1975, an announcement was made to say agreement had been reached in three areas, known as 'baskets'. Together these were known as the Helskinki Accords*.

Countries' borders are permanent. They cannot be changed by force.

We will try to improve relations between the East and West. We will make trade agreements and make a joint space mission.

We will respect human rights*. This includes freedom of speech and religion.

1. EUROPEAN BORDERS

2. INTERNATIONAL CO-OPERATION

3. HUMAN RIGHTS

Figure 3.2 The main agreements covered in the three 'baskets' of the Helsinki Accords.

Source C

The US–Soviet team of astronauts and cosmonauts that worked on the Apollo-Soyuz space mission of 1975.

What were the strengths of the treaty?	What were the weaknesses of the treaty?	What were the consequences of the treaty?
• Brezhnev was very pleased with the Basket 1 and Basket 2 agreements as they guaranteed the borders of the Soviet states. • The USA were very pleased with the Basket 3 agreement as they thought it would weaken communism.	• Some US politicians were angry that the Soviet state borders were guaranteed. • There was no way to make the Soviet Union follow Basket 3 and protect human rights. • The Soviet government was concerned that Basket 3 would weaken the Soviet Union.	• The Basket 1 agreement meant that the West accepted the borders of the Soviet states for the first time since the Second World War. • The Basket 2 agreement led to a joint US–Soviet space mission in 1975. • The accords showed some trust which helped the SALT 2 talks.

Source D

The Helsinki Accords were signed by President Gerald Ford on behalf of the USA. He made this statement upon signing the treaty.

History will judge this conference not by what we say here today, but by what we do tomorrow. Not by the promises we make, but by the promises we keep.

Source E

Comments made by the Soviet Ambassador Gromyko to the United Nations about the Helsinki Accords.

The members of the Politburo* read the full text. They had no objections when they read the first and second sections. When they got to the third 'humanitarian' section, their hair stood on end. Some said it was a complete betrayal of communist ideology. But Gromyko came up with this argument. The main thing about the Helsinki treaty is the recognition of the borders. That is what we shed our blood for in the Great Patriotic War*. All 35 signatories* are now saying these are the borders of Europe. As for human rights, Gromyko said, 'Well, who's the master of this house? We are the master and it will be up to us how we decide to act. Who can force us?'

Key terms

Politburo*

The name for the group of top politicians in the Soviet Union.

Great Patriotic War*

What the Soviet Union called the Second World War.

Signatories*

Countries that signed the Helsinki Accords.

SALT 2

After SALT 1, the USA and the Soviet Union tried to make a new agreement called SALT 2. This would put more limitations on nuclear weapons.

SALT (Strategic Arms Limitation Treaty) 2	
What was agreed?	• There were new limits on weapons like missile launchers and strategic bombers.
	• Testing or using new types of intercontinental ballistic missiles (ICBMs) was banned.

However, SALT 2 was never put into action. By the end of the 1970s, détente was failing for a number of reasons.

- US politicians and citizens did not trust the Soviet Union and believed that agreements with communist countries showed weakness.
- In November 1979, Islamic militants held Americans hostage in the US embassy* in Tehran*. Many Americans blamed détente for making them look weak, encouraging groups to attack Americans.
- President Carter's advisers asked him to act more strongly against the Soviet Union.
- In December 1979, the Soviet Union invaded Afghanistan. The US government refused to accept SALT 2 in response, and détente came to an end.

Key term

Embassy*

Countries send representatives to other countries to take part in negotiations. An embassy is also the building where diplomats work in another country.

Tehran*

The capital of Iran.

Ratify*

Accepting a treaty formally. If the Senate had ratified SALT 2, the terms would have become official US policy.

Activities ?

1 Why did the Helsinki Accords improve the relationship between the USA and the Soviet Union?

2 Afghanistan is a long way from the USA. Why would the Soviet invasion in 1979 make them refuse to ratify* the SALT 2 treaty?

Exam-style question, Section A

Write a narrative account analysing the key events of détente in the years 1970–79.

You may use the following in your answer:

- SALT 1, 1972
- The Helsinki Accords, 1975.

You **must** also use information of your own.   **8 marks**

Exam tip

A narrative account means telling the story of what happened. It needs the events in order. Good answers will show how one event led to another event.

To write a good narrative, focus on including the start, middle and end of the account.

Summary

- The events of the 1960s had worried world leaders about the threat of nuclear war.
- The arms race increased that worry.
- Both the USA and the Soviet Union had domestic reasons for wanting to improve relations.
- There was a series of agreements to limit nuclear weapons in the 1970s.
- By the end of the 1970s, the spirit of co-operation had died.

Checkpoint

Strengthen

S1 What was 'MAD'?

S2 What were the weaknesses of SALT 1?

S3 Why was SALT 2 not ratified by the USA?

Challenge

C1 What different aims did world leaders have in the Helsinki Accords?

How confident do you feel about your answers to these questions? Form a small group and discuss any questions you are not sure about. Look for the answers in this section. Now rewrite your answers as a group.

Learning outcomes

- Know why the Soviet Union invaded Afghanistan.
- Understand how the invasion affected international relations.
- Know about Ronald Reagan's role in the 'Second Cold War'.

Timeline

The 'Second Cold War', 1979–84

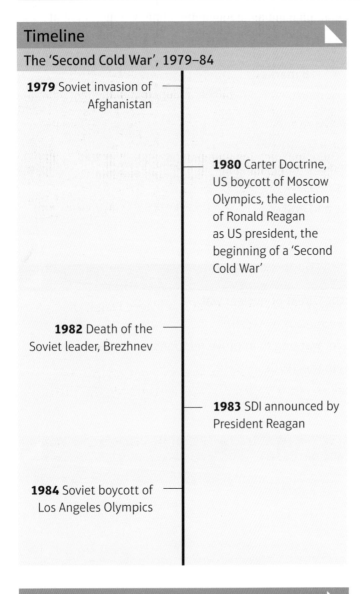

1979 Soviet invasion of Afghanistan

1980 Carter Doctrine, US boycott of Moscow Olympics, the election of Ronald Reagan as US president, the beginning of a 'Second Cold War'

1982 Death of the Soviet leader, Brezhnev

1983 SDI announced by President Reagan

1984 Soviet boycott of Los Angeles Olympics

Key terms

Shah*

King or emperor. Iran was ruled by shahs until the 1979 revolution.

Muslim fundamentalism*

Following very strict Islamic rules. This often includes trying to remove Western, non-Muslim influences on society.

The Soviet invasion of Afghanistan, 1979

Why was the Soviet Union interested in Afghanistan?

Afghanistan was an important neighbour to the Soviet Union. The countries got on well.

In 1979, there was a revolution in ~~Afghanistan~~ *Iran* and the Shah* was replaced by a Muslim fundamentalist* government. Moscow was determined not to let Muslim fundamentalism spread into the Soviet Union. They had many Muslim citizens. It was important to make sure that there was a pro-Soviet government in Afghanistan.

Figure 3.3 Afghanistan in 1979 and its borders with the Soviet Union, Pakistan and Iran.

Build-up to the invasion

In September 1979, Hafizullah Amin replaced the pro-Soviet Afghanistan government in a coup*. At first Moscow did nothing.

↓

Brezhnev heard rumours that the USA might offer help to Amin. He decided to act.

↓

In December 1979, Soviet troops invaded Afghanistan. The Soviet Union claimed that it was helping Amin against the mujahideen*.

↓

Three days later, Amin was murdered, probably by Soviet soldiers. He was replaced by Babrak Karmal, who was pro-Soviet.

↓

For the next ten years, Soviet troops stayed in Afghanistan fighting the mujahideen. It cost the Soviet Union $8 billion each year. About 15,000 Soviet soldiers died in the war. About 1.5 million Afghan civilians also died.

Figure: The invasion of Afghanistan, 1979–89.

The US reaction

Source A

Afghan mujahideen standing on a captured Soviet tank, 18 January 1980.

Key terms

Coup*

When a government or leader is replaced illegally, sometimes using violence.

Mujahideen*

Muslim fundamentalists in Afghanistan who fought against Hafizullah Amin and Soviet troops in the 1980s.

Economic sanctions*

Measures taken to damage a country's economy, usually involving a trade ban.

> The Soviet invasion of Afghanistan is the biggest threat to peace since the Second World War.

> We will not accept SALT 2. We will spend more money on our military.

> We will use force to stop any spread of Communism. This policy will be called the Carter Doctrine.

> We will place economic sanctions* on the Soviet Union, and send money and weapons to the mujahideen to help them fight.

US President Carter

> We are only protecting our own interests. Afghanistan is our neighbour.

Soviet leader Brezhnev

Figure: How the US viewed the Soviet invasion of Afghanistan.

The impact of the invasion on USA–Soviet relations

Détente was already nearly over by 1979. The invasion of Afghanistan destroyed any chance that it might work. Some historians think that US President Carter over-reacted to the invasion on purpose as a way to end détente.

In 1980, President Reagan was elected as US president. He said that the USA should stand up for itself and act tough against communism. He believed that communism was 'evil'. Because of the Afghanistan invasion, he won a landslide victory*.

> **Key terms**
>
> **Landslide victory***
>
> When a politician wins an election by winning many more votes than their opponent.
>
> **Consequences***
>
> The results or outcomes of an event. They can be positive or negative.

THINKING HISTORICALLY   Cause and Consequence (2c)

Far-reaching consequences*

Most events have many consequences. Their impact can often be felt in different areas. For example, an event could affect the economy, politics, international relations and society. The Soviet Union's decision to invade Afghanistan was a major event in the Cold War that had consequences in several different areas.

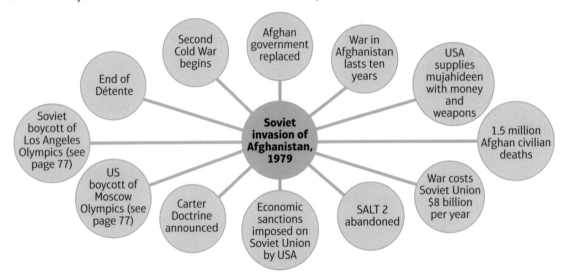

1 How many consequences are in this list? Can you think of any more consequences?

2 Sort the consequences into four groups: international relations, government, social, economic.

3 Which of the four groups of consequences do you think caused the most serious problems? Give one reason for your choice.

4 Which of these consequences do you think:

   a were intended by the Soviet Union when they invaded Afghanistan?

   b were not intended by the Soviet Union when they invaded Afghanistan?

The Olympic boycotts

In 1980, the Olympic Games were held in Moscow. The Soviet Union planned to use them to show off to all the audiences that would be watching around the world.

The USA decided to boycott* the Olympics. Over 60 other countries joined the boycott. The USA did this for two reasons:

- As a protest against the Soviet invasion of Afghanistan in 1979.
- To show how powerful the USA was because so many countries joined their boycott.

The boycott was effective. The number of top athletes who did not go to the Moscow Olympics made it look like a second rate event. The Soviet Union was furious.

This damaged international relations. Four years later, the 1984 Olympic Games were held in the USA. The Soviet Union boycotted them like the USA had in 1980 and 15 communist countries joined them.

Ronald Reagan and the 'Second Cold War'

Reagan's policies

President Reagan was much tougher towards the Soviet Union than previous presidents. This led to more hostility that is often known as the 'Second Cold War'.

Key term

Boycott*

Refusing to do something, like attend an event, as a protest.

US President Reagan

Figure: The Reagan Doctrine

The Strategic Defense Initiative

President Reagan knew that the Soviet economy was struggling. By giving money to anti-communist groups, he hoped to force the Soviet Union to spend more money fighting them. He thought the Soviet Union would struggle financially.

In 1983, Reagan announced a new policy called the Strategic Defense Initiative (SDI), which most people called 'Star Wars'. Satellites with lasers which could shoot down Soviet missiles would be placed in orbit around the Earth.

The truth was that this technology was not ready, but Reagan spoke as though it was.

The Soviet Union was shocked. It believed that the SDI was almost ready to be used. It knew that:

- SDI would mean that it could not attack the USA with missiles, but the USA could still attack the Soviet Union.
- All the money the Soviet Union had spent on missiles would be wasted if SDI was real.
- It could not afford to build its own version of SDI.

Because the Soviet Union believed Reagan's announcement about SDI, it had to start thinking about ways of ending its arms race with the USA.

Source B

Ronald Reagan announcing SDI in a televised address to the nation on 23 March 1983.

Activities ?

1   Look at Source B. What does the photograph on the easel behind Reagan show?

2   Source B is a photo of Reagan announcing SDI to the American people on television. Suggest reasons why the photograph on the easel has been placed there.

3   a   What was the Soviet reaction to the announcement of SDI?

    b   Why did SDI have such a major impact on relations between the USA and Soviet Union?

Exam-style question, Section A

Explain the importance of the Soviet invasion of Afghanistan for relations between the USA and the Soviet Union.   **8 marks**

Source C

An extract from Ronald Reagan's autobiography*, published in 1990.

During the late seventies, I felt our country had begun to abdicate* its historical role as the spiritual leader of the Free World* and its foremost defender of democracy... Predictably, the Soviets had interpreted our hesitation as reluctance to act and had tried to exploit it in their agenda to achieve a communist-dominated world... I deliberately set out to say some frank things about the Soviets to let them know there were some new fellows in Washington.

Key terms

Autobiography*

An account of a person's life that they wrote themselves.

Abdicate*

To step down from office or power.

Free World*

A term used by the West for countries not under communist rule. It suggested that people living under communism were not free.

Exam tip

The question asks about importance. That means that you need to explain why it was important, or why the event mattered. What did it affect?

You need to make sure that you focus on the area mentioned in the question – relations between the USA and the Soviet Union. You should only write about that. For example, if you write about other areas, like why the Soviet Union invaded, you will not get marks. Explain how the invasion affected relations. Did it make them better or worse?

Summary

- The Soviet Union was concerned about Muslim fundamentalism in Afghanistan.
- The USA saw the Soviet invasion of Afghanistan as spreading communism.
- Relations between the USA and the Soviet Union worsened.
- Ronald Reagan was elected with a 'get tough on the communists' policy.
- A 'Second Cold War' began.

Checkpoint

Strengthen

S1 Who were the mujahideen?

S2 What was the Carter Doctrine?

S3 Explain how 'SDI' was supposed to work.

Challenge

C1 How was Reagan's attitude to the Soviet Union different to that of previous presidents?

How confident do you feel about your answers to these questions? Form a small group and discuss any questions you are not sure about. Look for the answers in this section. Now rewrite your answers as a group.

3.3 The collapse of Soviet control in Eastern Europe, 1985–91

Learning outcomes

- Understand the impact of the arms race on the Soviet economy.
- Know about Gorbachev's 'new thinking' and its impact on international relations.
- Know about the end of the Cold War and the break-up of the Soviet Union.

Timeline

End of the Cold War and the Soviet Union, 1985–91

1985 Gorbachev becomes Soviet leader, Geneva Summit

1986 Reykjavik Summit

1987 Intermediate-Range Nuclear Force Treaty (INF)

1988 Moscow Summit

1989 Fall of Berlin Wall

1990 Gorbachev wins Nobel Prize

1991 Gorbachev overthrown, Soviet Union dissolves

Key terms

Bankrupt*

When a country or company has run out of money.

Unrest*

When people protest.

Martial law*

When a government uses the military to keep control.

Gorbachev's new thinking

Mikhail Gorbachev became leader of the Soviet Union in March 1985. At this time, the Soviet Union was facing a number of serious problems.

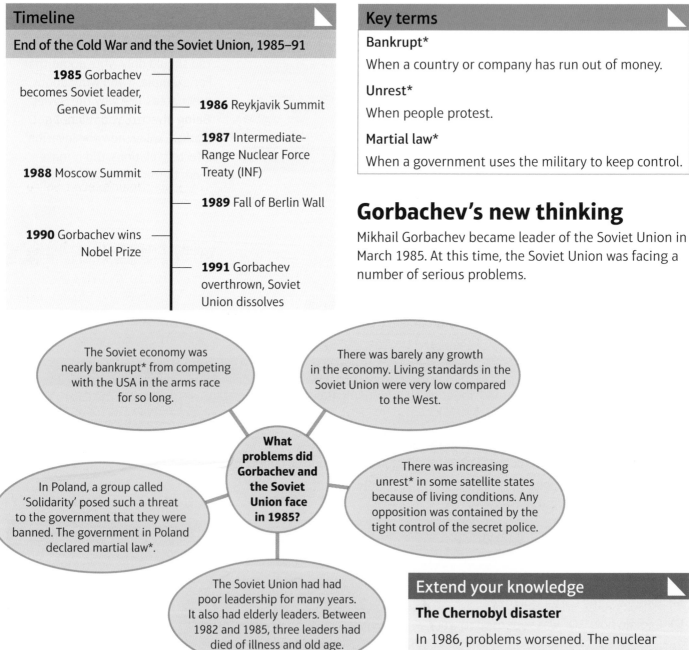

Figure: Problems faced by the Soviet Union in 1985.

The Soviet economy was nearly bankrupt* from competing with the USA in the arms race for so long.

There was barely any growth in the economy. Living standards in the Soviet Union were very low compared to the West.

What problems did Gorbachev and the Soviet Union face in 1985?

There was increasing unrest* in some satellite states because of living conditions. Any opposition was contained by the tight control of the secret police.

In Poland, a group called 'Solidarity' posed such a threat to the government that they were banned. The government in Poland declared martial law*.

The Soviet Union had had poor leadership for many years. It also had elderly leaders. Between 1982 and 1985, three leaders had died of illness and old age.

Extend your knowledge

The Chernobyl disaster

In 1986, problems worsened. The nuclear reactor at Chernobyl, in what is now Ukraine, exploded, spreading radiation. 350,000 people had to be evacuated and even now no one can live in the area. It was a huge embarrassment for the Soviet Union.

Gorbachev knew that things had to change and he said, 'We can't go on living like this.' He wanted to fix communism in the Soviet Union so he made some new policies.

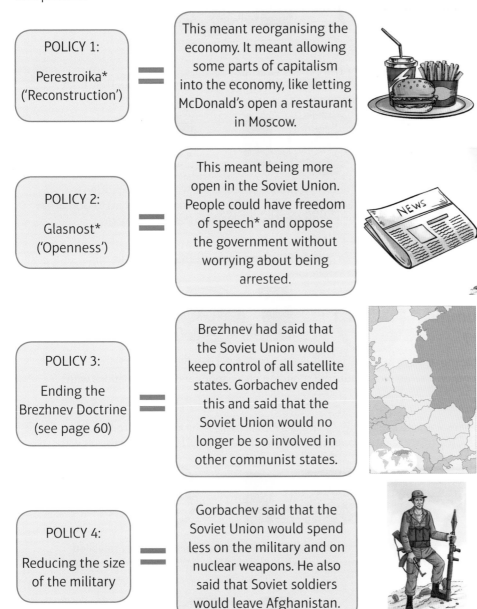

POLICY 1:

Perestroika*
('Reconstruction')

=

This meant reorganising the economy. It meant allowing some parts of capitalism into the economy, like letting McDonald's open a restaurant in Moscow.

POLICY 2:

Glasnost*
('Openness')

=

This meant being more open in the Soviet Union. People could have freedom of speech* and oppose the government without worrying about being arrested.

POLICY 3:

Ending the Brezhnev Doctrine (see page 60)

=

Brezhnev had said that the Soviet Union would keep control of all satellite states. Gorbachev ended this and said that the Soviet Union would no longer be so involved in other communist states.

POLICY 4:

Reducing the size of the military

=

Gorbachev said that the Soviet Union would spend less on the military and on nuclear weapons. He also said that Soviet soldiers would leave Afghanistan.

Figure: The policies of Gorbachev.

Key terms

Perestroika*

Russian for 'reconstruction'. It was Gorbachev's plan for reorganising and restructuring the Soviet state. and economy

Glasnost*

Russian for 'openness' or 'transparency'. It was Gorbachev's new, more open, attitude to government and foreign relations.

Freedom of speech*

Being able to say or write an opinion without fear of arrest.

KGB*

The Soviet Union's secret police force.

Source A

A joke from the Soviet era.

A frightened man came to the KGB*.

'My talking parrot has disappeared.'

'That's not the kind of case we handle. Go and make a report at the police station.'

'Excuse me, of course I know that I need to talk to the police. I've come here to make an official statement that I completely disagree with the parrot.'

The US response

Gorbachev's new policies caused a change of thinking in the USA. Reagan had started as a president who was tough on communism. He had spent more on weapons and been aggressive to the Soviet Union. When Gorbachev became Soviet leader in 1985, Reagan saw that Gorbachev was willing to make changes. Reagan wanted to work with Gorbachev to bring the Cold War to an end.

Gorbachev's new thinking in action

During the first four years of Gorbachev's leadership of the Soviet Union, important steps were made to limit nuclear weapons.

Geneva Summit November 1985

At Geneva, Gorbachev and Reagan met for the first time.

Outcome

No formal agreements but Reagan and Gorbachev established a good working relationship. They both wanted to improve relations between their countries.

Reykjavik Summit October 1986

Gorbachev was worried about the danger that nuclear weapons posed to the world. The explosion in 1986 at the Soviet Chernobyl nuclear power station probably made this seem more important to Gorbachev. In Reykjavik, Gorbachev offered to reduce nuclear weapons if the US gave up their SDI program.

Outcome

Both leaders knew that the US could not agree to give up SDI. Once again, the meeting broke up with no formal agreement but an improvement in relations.

Washington Summit December 1987

Gorbachev accepted that the US were not going to scrap SDI. He realised that his country's best interests lay in agreements on disarmament, reducing spending on weapons and better relations with the West.

Outcome

This was the first US–Soviet summit to lead to the signing of a formal treaty – the Intermediate-Range Nuclear Force (INF) Treaty. The treaty said that both countries would remove all land-based missiles with a range of 500–5,500 km.

Moscow Summit 1988

In this summit, some extra details in the INF treaty were agreed. Later in the year, Gorbachev travelled to the USA. He announced that the Soviet Union would reduce the number of Warsaw Pact troops and stop fighting in Afghanistan.

Malta Summit 1989

At Malta, Gorbachev met with the new president of the USA, George Bush.

Outcome

No new agreements were made, but both the USA and the Soviet Union saw this meeting as marking the end of the Cold War.

Gorbachev said, 'I assure the President of the United States that I will never start a hot war against the USA.' Bush said, 'We can realise a lasting peace and transform the East–West relationship to one of enduring co-operation.'

Figure 3.4 The main summits in the 1980s. Summits were meetings between the US and Soviet leaders.

Source B

Reagan and Gorbachev sign the INF Treaty in Washington, in December 1987.

The end of the Soviet hold on Eastern Europe

Once Gorbachev had announced that the Soviet Union was giving up the Brezhnev Doctrine (see page 60), the Soviet satellite countries were free to choose how they would be governed. They would no longer have to fear that the Soviets would step in as they had in Hungary in 1956 (see page 32) and Czechoslovakia in 1968 (see page 58). Gorbachev's reforms, like introducing more openness to government, encouraged the people of the satellite states to believe that they could make changes to improve their standard of living and freedom.

Key term

Free election*

Elections where different parties can be elected, not just communists.

June 1989: Poland
A non-communist party, Solidarity, is elected in Poland.

September 1989: East Germany
Huge numbers of East Germans start leaving to live in the West. No-one stops them.

October 1989: East Germany
Protests start against the Communist government. Gorbachev says that the Soviet Union will not stop the protests.

November 1989: East Germany
The border between East and West Germany is opened. People are allowed to leave. People on both sides start to pull the Berlin Wall down.

May 1989: Hungary
The fence between Hungary and Austria is removed. New free elections* are arranged.

November 1989: Czechoslovakia
The communist government is overthrown and replaced by an anti-communist leader.

December 1989: Romania
The communist leader is overthrown and executed.

December 1989: Bulgaria
The communist leader resigns. Free elections are arranged.

December 1990: Yugoslavia
Free elections are arranged. Yugoslavia breaks up into four smaller countries.

Figure 3.5 The end of communist rule in Eastern Europe.

Source D

A German, who was a 10-year-old living in East Germany when the Berlin Wall fell, describes visiting West Germany three months later.

I went with my mother by train from Berlin. I remember the day very well; being excited and also a little nervous. We passed the border, and no one asked us for our passports or where we wanted to go – unimaginable only months earlier. We arrived and everything looked and felt different. Streets were clean, buildings and houses were kept well and the air did not smell of burnt brown coal. For a few days I felt like I was living in a different world. I returned home after a few days, and became aware of the large differences between East and West, in particular of the rundown, sad and dirty state that East Germany was in.

Gorbachev did not want to end communism. His reforms were supposed to end the Cold War. But they caused the end of communism in Eastern Europe and the collapse of the Soviet Union.

The significance of the fall of the Berlin Wall

When the Berlin Wall came down on 9 November 1989, many people were happy. They could see family and friends for the first time in 30 years. Many people took pieces of the wall as souvenirs.

The fall of the Wall was important politically because of the message that it sent to the world. It showed that communism was failing across Eastern Europe. More importantly, it showed that the Soviet Union would not step in to stop countries abandoning communism.

The Berlin Wall had represented the Cold War in Europe. The collapse of the Berlin Wall represented the end of the Cold War.

The end of the Warsaw Pact

The Warsaw Pact had been formed after the Western Allies set up NATO (see Chapter 1). The Warsaw Pact had been the way that the Soviet Union controlled the communist countries in Eastern Europe. For example, they had used the Warsaw Pact to control Hungary in 1956 and Czechoslovakia in 1968.

When the communist governments in Eastern Europe ended, it was impossible to keep the Warsaw Pact going. It came to an end in 1991.

Source C

East Berliners climbing on the Wall on 11 November 1989.

Europe was reunited
The Warsaw Pact had split Europe into two. When it ended, it showed that the East–West divide between capitalism and communism was gone. The 'Iron Curtain*' had gone.

Gorbachev fell from power
Gorbachev had not intended to end communism. When the Warsaw Pact ended, he looked weak. Hard-line Communists* blamed him for losing control. In 1991, his opponents tried to remove him from power. They failed but his reputation was damaged. He resigned on 25 December 1991. The Soviet Union broke up into separate states immediately afterwards

What were the consequences of the Warsaw Pact ending?

End of military threat to the West
The Warsaw Pact had been the Soviet Union's military alliance. Without it, there was no armed force facing the USA and NATO. The Cold War was over.

The satellite states regained their independence
The Warsaw Pact was what the Soviet Union used to control Soviet satellite states. Without it, states did not need to obey the Soviet Union or run their economy for the Soviet Union. When the Warsaw Pact ended, every single member abandoned communism.

Figure: Impact of the end of the Warsaw Pact.

Source E

Boris Yeltsin, president of the Russian republic, standing on top of a tank in August 1989. He is rallying support for Gorbachev. One of his supporters is waving a Russian flag.

Key terms

Iron Curtain*

The nickname for the divide in Europe between East and West during the Cold War.

Hard-line Communists*

Committed Communist politicians who did not like the idea of weakening communism.

Activity ?

In a small group, decide which of these two statements you agree with more.

a 'The Cold War came to an end because President Reagan's policies won it for the USA.'

b 'The Cold War came to an end because Mikhail Gorbachev was a weak leader.'

As a group, find as many reasons as you can to support the statement that you have chosen. You need to be ready to share your evidence with the class.

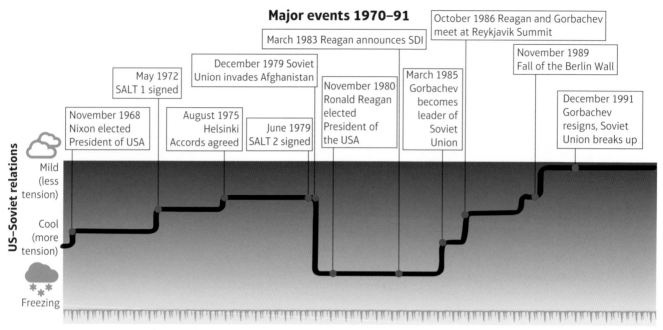

Figure 3.6 Relations between the USA and Soviet Union, 1968–91.

Exam-style question, Section A ⬤

Explain **two** consequences of Mikhail Gorbachev's decision to abandon the Brezhnev Doctrine.   **8 marks**

Exam tip ⬤

This question asks about 'consequences'. This means the outcomes or results. So you don't need to write about how or why the Doctrine was abandoned. Instead, focus on what difference abandoning it made. How did this change things? Think about how countries in Eastern Europe reacted to hearing that the Brezhnev Doctrine had ended.

Summary ◥

- The weakness of the Soviet economy led to a rethink of the country's role in international politics.
- Gorbachev's 'new thinking' encouraged a positive response from the USA.
- The Soviet Union abandoned the Brezhnev Doctrine.
- Nationalist uprisings resulted in the break-up of the Warsaw Pact.
- The Soviet Union broke up into separate states.

Checkpoint ◥

Strengthen

S1 When did Reagan and Gorbachev meet in Geneva?

S2 What was Gorbachev's 'new thinking'?

S3 What were *perestroika* and *glasnost*?

Challenge

C1 Why was the fall of the Berlin Wall so important?

How confident do you feel about your answers to these questions? Re-read the chapter, making notes as you go. Now try answering the questions again.

Recap: The end of the Cold War, 1970–91

Recall quiz

1 When were the Helsinki Accords signed?
2 What event led to President Carter announcing the Carter Doctrine?
3 How did the Soviet Union pay back the USA for boycotting the 1980 Olympics?
4 In which Warsaw Pact country was martial law declared in 1981?
5 What was SDI?
6 Why were there four Soviet leaders between 1982 and 1985?
7 What was the main agreement of the INF Treaty?
8 What happened in Germany in November 1989?
9 What happened to Gorbachev after the Warsaw Pact ended in 1991?
10 When did Gorbachev resign?

Activities   ?

1 Write a short paragraph explaining why détente came to an end from 1979. Your paragraph should include two reasons.
2 Why is the period 1979–85 sometimes called the 'Second Cold War'?
3 How did Gorbachev's new thinking, like glasnost and perestroika, lead to ending the Cold War? What is the link?

Exam-style question, Section A

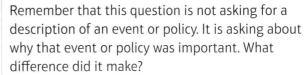

Explain **two** of the following:

- the importance of the nuclear arms race for relations between the USA and the Soviet Union
- the importance of the Soviet invasion of Afghanistan for relations between the USA and the Soviet Union
- the importance of Ronald Reagan for relations between the USA and the Soviet Union.   **16 marks**

Exam tip

Remember that this question is not asking for a description of an event or policy. It is asking about why that event or policy was important. What difference did it make?

Remember to pay attention to the context. All three questions are about relations between the USA and the Soviet Union. So you do not need to spend time writing about the impact of the invasion of Afghanistan on the people who lived there, for example.

Writing historically: narrative analysis

When you write a narrative analysis, you need to explain a series of events. This means showing the **causes** and **effects**, or consequences, of an event. You need to be able to link the causes and effects together.

Learning objectives

By the end of this lesson, you will understand how to:

- use simple connecting words to link points
- use connecting words which show the relationship between two ideas.

Definitions

Simple connections: words that link two ideas together, for example, 'and', 'but', 'so', 'or'.

Analytical connections: a linking word that helps us to understand the relationship between the ideas, for example, 'because', 'consequently', 'although', 'if'.

Narrative explanation: this means explaining the story of an event by linking its parts to show the causes and effects.

How can I link my points in sentences to show cause and effect?

When explaining complex sequences of events, we need to use linking words to create sentences which connect ideas. Look at this exam-style task which needs narrative explanation.

> Write a narrative account analysing the key events of the Soviet invasion of Afghanistan.
>
> **(8 marks)**

1. How could you link these four points using simple connecting words? You should use words such as 'and', 'but' and 'so'.

> In 1978 the pro-Soviet government in Afghanistan was overthrown in a local coup.
>
> The Soviet Union learned that the new government was in talks with the USA.
>
> The Soviet Union was worried about losing influence in the region.
>
> They invaded Afghanistan in December 1979.

Although using linking words is good, for a narrative explanation you need to use words that show how the ideas are connected. For example, have a look at how you could link the same sentences with better connecting words that show how the ideas are connected:

> In 1978 the pro-Soviet government in Afghanistan was overthrown in a local coup. Later, the Soviet Union learned that the new government was in talks with the USA, which caused the Soviet Union to worry about losing influence in the region. In response, they invaded Afghanistan in December 1979.

This language is now starting to be more specific about how the ideas are connected together. For example, the last sentence starts with 'in response'. This shows that the invasion was a direct result of the worry that the Soviet Union had about their influence in Afghanistan.

Did you notice that the connecting words were not only used in the middle of sentences? You can also use these words to start sentences.

Showing the right relationship between ideas

2. The right linking word will show the right relationship. For each pair of sentences below, rewrite them into one sentence that has the right type of linking words.

   a. Connect these two sentences to show an explanation (showing the cause and effect). You could use words such as 'because', 'as', 'in order that'.

   The Soviet Union wanted to have a pro-Soviet government in Afghanistan. *It did not want hardline Muslim ideology to spread to the Soviet Union.*

   b. Connect these two sentences to show a condition (one thing happened as long as another thing was happening). You could use words such as 'if', 'unless', 'while', 'since'.

   The Soviet Union was concerned about Hafizullah Amin and his government in Afghanistan. *Brezhnev had heard rumours he was in talks with the USA.*

   c. Connect these two sentences to show a comparison (where two ideas are similar or opposite). You could use words such as 'although', 'whereas', 'despite', 'however'.

   The Soviet Union said they had been invited by Amin to help him deal with terrorism. *They made a full military invasion of Afghanistan and put in a new leader.*

   d. Connect these two sentences to show a sequence (the order of events). You could use words such as 'when', 'as', 'before', 'after', 'until', 'subsequently'.

   Hafizullah Amin was killed. *He was replaced by the pro-Soviet Babrak Karmal.*

Improving an answer

Now look at this paragraph from the beginning of one student's response to the narrative analysis task on the previous page.

> In 1978 the pro-Soviet government in Afghanistan was toppled in a coup. In the following year there was a revolution in Iran. This brought in a new Muslim fundamentalist government. This worried the Soviets. They did not want fundamentalist ideas spreading to the Muslim population in the Soviet Union. They were also worried about losing influence in Afghanistan when the new ruler Hafizullah Amin held talks with the US government.

3. Try rewriting this paragraph by linking together the ideas. Make the order of events, and the relationship between cause and effect, clear.

4. Now add a second paragraph to the answer in the same style. You could next mention the events of the invasion. Try starting with this line:

> The Soviet Union invaded Afghanistan in December 1979. Although they claimed ...

Writing analytical narrative

The difference between a story and a narrative account that analyses

Paper 2, Question 2 will ask you to 'Write a narrative account analysing…' (see page 95 in *Preparing for your exams*). This does not mean just writing a story. It means explaining how events are linked together in order.

To write a narrative analysis, you must:

- show how one event caused another event or made a change to something else
- show how the events in the narrative account are linked together in a sequence*.

It is the way that you link the events together that is important.

Narratives for young children are always stories. They describe what happened. For example, the book *The Wind in the Willows* has stories about Toad of Toad Hall. These narratives show how Toad got himself into a number of scrapes. One story describes his obsession with fast cars, then him stealing one, then him being arrested, and finally him being sent to prison.

Here is a short part of *The Wind in the Willows*.

Toad steals a motor car

Toad had a passion for cars. He saw a car in the middle of the yard, quite unattended. Toad walked slowly round it. 'I wonder,' he said to himself, 'if this car starts easily?' Next moment he was turning the starting handle. Then he heard the sound of the engine and, as if in a dream, he found himself in the driver's seat. He drove the car out through the archway and the car leapt forward through the open country…

This has the first part of a narrative: a sequence of events in the right order. The author used words and phrases like 'next moment' and 'then' to show the sequence.

So what is missing? There are no analytical links between events. The author could have used words like 'because', 'in order to' or 'as a result of this'.

For example:

Toad saw the car parked in the middle of the yard. Because there was no one with it, he took the opportunity to have a good look at it. He even gave the starting handle a turn in order to see how easily it started. It started easily, but the sound of the engine affected Toad so much that his old passion for cars resurfaced and his urge to drive the car increased to such an extent that it became irresistible. As a result, as if in a dream, he found himself in the driver's seat…

The new linking words make it clear what difference each step made. And process words* show something was happening. In this example, the process words and phrases are 'affected', 'resurfaced', 'increased' and 'became'.

Activities   ?

1 Choose a story that you know well – or make up a story of your own.

2 a Select up to six key events in the story. Your events should be from the beginning, middle and end of the story.

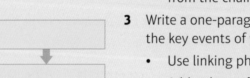

   b Create a flow chart with arrows from one event to the next in the sequence, like this.

   c Label your arrows with linking phrases* chosen from the chain of linkages (see Figure 1).

3 Write a one-paragraph narrative account analysing the key events of your story.

   - Use linking phrases.
   - Add at least **three** process words. (You can find ideas in the process word case in Figure 2, or choose your own.)

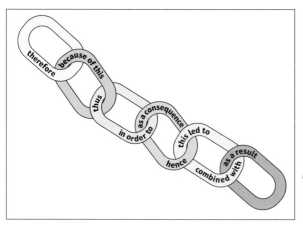

Figure 1 The chain of linkages

Figure 2 Process word case

Writing historical accounts analysing...

You may be asked to write an account that analyses the key events which led to something, or the key events of a crisis, or the way in which something developed. This example has shown the skills you will need to write a good historical account. As you prepare for your examination, you should practise by:

- selecting key events
- writing them in sequence*
- linking them into a process that explains an outcome*.

As you study the events of the Cold War, note the linking phrases* and process words* the author has used in this book. When you create your own analytical historical narratives, try to make use of both linking phrases and process words.

Activities ?

Study the timeline on page 20. You can use the events from it to help you to answer the following question:

Write a narrative account analysing the development of Europe into two blocs* in the years 1947–49

1   With a partner, write the events on pieces of card, without their dates, and then:

   a   sort them into the correct order; then jumble them up again and sort them into order a second time

   b   decide what the attitude was that was changing throughout these events. (Hint: how did the Soviet Union and the USA view each other?)

2   Working by yourself, write a one-paragraph narrative account. Focus on what it is you are explaining: the creation of the two blocs in the Cold War. Aim to use four linking phrases and three process words.

3   Either swap accounts with a partner or check your own account.

   a   Highlight linking phrases in yellow.

   b   Highlight process words in green.

   c   Can you find a way to add one more linking phrase or process word to the paragraph?

You are now ready to complete your exam question. Remember to use **SSLaP**.

- **S**elect key events.
- **S**equence them in the right order.
- **L**ink them, **a**nd
- Use **P**rocess words to show what had changed in the outcome.

Preparing for your GCSE Paper 2 exam

Paper 2 overview

Paper 2 has two sections. Section A will be your questions on Superpower Relations and the Cold War (your Period Study). These are worth 20% of your GCSE History assessment. The whole exam is 1 hour 45 minutes. You should use 50 minutes to do Section A. That will leave time for Section B, which is your British Depth Study.

History Paper 2	Period Study and British Depth Study			Time 1 hour 45 mins
Section A	Period Study	Answer 3 questions	32 marks	50 minutes
Section B	Depth Options B1 or B2	Answer 3 questions	32 marks	55 minutes

Period Study Option 26 / 27: Superpower relations and the Cold War, 1941–91

You will answer Questions 1, 2 and 3.

1 Explain two consequences of... (2 x 4 marks)

- Time – 10 minutes
- What – explain two consequences.
- Length – up to half a page on each consequence.
- Focus – on the consequence or outcomes.
- Helpful phrases – 'as a result', 'as a consequence', 'the effect was'.
- Hints – keep it brief. Don't add extra information on extra lines.

2 Write a narrative account analysing... (8 marks)

- Time – 15 minutes.
- What – a narrative analysis that links events and shows how they led to an outcome. The question will have two hint bullet points.
- Length – up to two pages, but you do not have to use all the space.
- Focus – on linking events together to explain an outcome.
- Helpful phrases – the linking phrases and process words on page 91.
- Hints – focus on getting the events in the right order. It should have a beginning, middle and end.

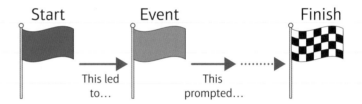

3 Explain two of the following... (2 x 8 marks)

- Time – 25 minutes.
- What – an explanation of how an event was important.
- Length – one page per event.
- Focus – showing how the event was important, or in other words, 'What difference did it make?'
- Helpful phrases – 'this caused', 'this led to', 'this was important because'.
- Hints – remember that you pick two out of the three options to answer. Make sure that your reason for saying it is important is clear.

Paper 2, Question 1

Explain **two** consequences of the decisions made by The Grand Alliance at the Yalta Conference in February 1945. **(8 marks)**

Exam tip

The question wants you to explain the results of an event. Try to not just describe the event. What difference did it make? What happened as a result?

Remember that consequences can be positive or negative.

Basic answer

Consequence 1:
They divided Germany into different parts. Each part had a different country in charge.

This answer has shown a correct consequence. But it is not specific. For example, it could say how many parts and which countries were in charge.

Consequence 2:
They could not agree about Poland or Eastern Europe. They had different opinions about elections so afterward there was tension.

This is also a true consequence. It could be more specific by saying what the different opinions were between the West and East about elections, and why it caused tension afterward.

Judgement

This is a basic answer. The student knows the basic consequences. But it is not very specific. It needs more detail. Use the feedback to rewrite this answer, making as many improvements as you can.

Paper 2, Question 1

Explain **two** consequences of the decisions made by The Grand Alliance at the Yalta Conference in February 1945. **(8 marks)**

Exam tip

To avoid just describing, you could try using sentences that start like this: 'As a result of this event…', 'The effect of this was…', 'This led to…'

Good answer

7th

Consequence 1:
As a result of the Yalta Conference, Germany was divided into different zones. There were four of these governed by different countries, like the USA. This division led to a lot of difficulties in the future.

This answer has identified a consequence and given a brief description. There is some detail. It could be improved further by adding more detail to provide an effective explanation. For example, which other countries owned zones, and what difficulties were caused?

Consequence 2:
Another consequence of the conference was that there was disagreement about how Poland was to be governed. It was agreed that there would be a government decided by free elections, but there was disagreement about who The Grand Alliance wanted to win those elections. This led to further tension.

This is a second correct consequence, and gives some better details about what happened and why. However, the second sentence does not explain fully how the decision led to disagreements between different members of The Grand Alliance. Why were free elections such a problem?

Judgement

This is a good answer because it identifies two consequences with some support. It could be made better by adding more explanation of consequences with specific information. Use the feedback to rewrite this answer, making as many improvements as you can.

Paper 2, Question 2

Write a narrative account analysing the key events leading to the break-up of the Warsaw Pact in the years 1985–91. You may use the following in your answer:

- Gorbachev became leader of the Soviet Union in 1985
- the fall of the Berlin Wall in 1989.

You **must** also use information of your own. **(8 marks)**

Exam tip

The key to answering this question is to first decide what main events led to the outcome. In this question, the outcome is the break-up of the Warsaw Pact. You can use the two bullet points to help you decide what to include. How did the events lead to the outcome? Put the events in the right sequence and link them together.

Basic answer

When Gorbachev came to power in the Soviet Union he had new ideas. He wanted to be more relaxed in how he ran the country. So then other countries that were communist started to think that they could make changes. This made some of the satellite states start to make changes, like East Germany. Then the Berlin Wall came down. Because of all of these things, the Warsaw Pact came to an end because no one was using it any more. Gorbachev couldn't stop it.

This has the basic events but without any detail to make it clearer.

Judgement

This is a basic answer. It does show some understanding of the basic narrative of events, but without any good examples or detail. The linking language is also basic. To improve, this answer needs better examples, more details and more linking phrases and process words. Use the feedback to rewrite this answer, making as many improvements as you can.

Paper 2, Question 2

Write a narrative account analysing the key events leading to the break-up of the Warsaw Pact in the years 1985–91. You may use the following in your answer:

- Gorbachev became leader of the Soviet Union in 1985
- the fall of the Berlin Wall in 1989.

You **must** also use information of your own. **(8 marks)**

Exam tip

Remember to link the events in order with phrases such as: 'this led to', 'as a result', 'as a consequence'. Then add process words such as: 'grew', 'worsened' or 'increased'. You can find other examples of these words on page 91.

7th

Good answer

When Gorbachev came to power in the Soviet Union he had a new way of thinking. He abandoned the Brezhnev Doctrine. There was more openness in the Soviet Union's government. This was noticed in the Soviet satellite countries and they began to break away from the control of the Soviet Union. First of all, East Germans started leaving for the West through Hungary. No one stopped them. So then Poland had free elections and the communists lost. As a result of these new ideas of freedom, the Berlin Wall came down in November and there was a revolution in Czechoslovakia. This meant they were no longer communist. In July 1991 the Warsaw Pact was dissolved because it no longer had a purpose.

This answer has listed the main events so the sequence of events is right. It could be improved further by showing more clearly how each event led to the next event, and providing more detail.

Judgement

This is a good answer because it shows the main events in the narrative account. The events are in the correct sequence and it has some linking phrases. It could be improved further by adding process words. For example, how did the openness in the Soviet Union lead to the satellite states starting to try to break away? How did this lead to the Berlin Wall coming down? The links need to be clearer. Use the feedback to rewrite this answer, making as many improvements as you can.

Paper 2, Question 3

Explain **two** of the following:

- The importance of the Truman Doctrine for international relations after the Second World War.
- The importance of the building of the Berlin Wall for the development of the Cold War.
- The importance of the Olympic boycotts for relations between the USA and the Soviet Union. **(16 marks)**

The sample answer below covers just the bullet point about the Olympic boycotts. Don't forget in the exam you need to write about two.

Exam tip

This question is about importance, but you need to read the second part of the question because it tells you what you need to focus on. For example, the third bullet point on the Olympic boycotts says '**for** relations between the USA and the Soviet Union'. Don't just describe the events of the Olympic boycotts. Make sure you focus on how it changed things **for** relations between the USA and the Soviet Union.

Basic answer

The Olympic boycotts was where the USA persuaded other countries not to go to the Olympics in Moscow. This was important because it upset the Soviet Union. They were angry that they had prepared the Olympics and spent lots of money on them to look good and there were lots of countries like the USA that did not even go. This made the relationship worse between the two countries.

This paragraph is correct in saying that it was important because it damaged the relationship but it does not clearly explain how.

But the boycott was also important because it made the President of the USA look stronger. It made him more popular with Americans because they liked to see their president standing up to the Soviet Union.

Unfortunately, an examiner will not give marks for this paragraph because the question is about the relationship between the USA and the Soviet Union, not what the American public thought.

Judgement

This is a basic answer. It has started to say how the US boycott of the Moscow Olympics was important. But it needs to explain with more specific knowledge why it damaged the relationship, and how this made tensions worse in the Cold War. Use the feedback to rewrite this answer, making as many improvements as you can.

Paper 2, Question 3

Explain **two** of the following:

- The importance of the Truman Doctrine for international relations after the Second World War.
- The importance of the building of the Berlin Wall for the development of the Cold War.
- The importance of the Olympic boycotts for relations between the USA and the Soviet Union. **(16 marks)**

Exam tip

To avoid describing the event, try to use phrases such as: 'This was important because…', 'The impact of this was…', 'This led to a positive/negative change because…'

The sample answer below covers just the bullet point about the Olympic boycotts. Don't forget in the exam you need to write about two.

Good answer

The Olympic boycotts were very important. At this time relations between the USA and the Soviet Union were getting worse, even though there had been détente in the 1970s. The situation became even worse when the Soviet Union invaded Afghanistan. So the USA wanted a way to punish the Soviet Union. They did this by persuading lots of countries not to attend the Moscow Olympics in 1980. That really upset the Soviet Union because it was hoping to use the Olympics to show everyone how great communism was and how successful athletes from Warsaw Pact countries were. This would prove that communist society was better. Because the USA boycotted against the Soviet Union, it showed that détente was definitely over. This was important because in the 1980s there was a Second Cold War.

The Soviet Union was really upset about the boycott and got its revenge four years later when it led a boycott of the Olympics being held in Los Angeles. So the Cold War got colder.

This answer has correctly identified that the boycotts were important in intensifying the Cold War and explained why the boycott upset the Soviet Union.

The writer uses 'really upset' twice. It would be better to go into more depth about how the Soviet Union reacted.

Judgement

This is a good answer because in the first paragraph, it shows how the 1980 boycott damaged the relationship between East and West which had been getting better in the 1970s. The answer could be improved, however. It does not explain any link between the importance of the boycott and the Second Cold War. Also it does not give enough detail about the 1984 boycott to show the damage it did to the relationship between the USA and the Soviet Union. Use the feedback to rewrite this answer, making as many improvements as you can.

Answers to Recall Quiz questions

Chapter 1

1 Soviet Union, USA, Britain
2 Tehran – 1943, Yalta – 1945, Potsdam – 1945
3 Stalin, Roosevelt, Churchill, then: Stalin, Truman, Attlee
4 Truman said the spread of communism should be stopped and the USA would help countries that did not want to become communist
5 A state that is under the control of another state. Satellite states in Eastern Europe were controlled by the Soviet Union
6 Britain, France, USA and nine others
7 Soviet Union, Poland, Czechoslovakia, Hungary, Romania, Bulgaria, Albania, East Germany
8 1949
9 Inter-continental ballistic missile
10 Khrushchev

Chapter 2

1 Because Germany was occupied by the Soviets from the East and the democratic allies from the West. The country was divided into zones and so was the capital, Berlin
2 Large numbers of educated people were leaving East Germany for the West
3 Eisenhower, Kennedy, Johnson, Nixon
4 Khrushchev, Brezhnev
5 To show support for the people of West Berlin
6 1959
7 An attempt to topple Castro's government using CIA-trained Cuban exiles
8 Test Ban Treaty (1963), Outer Space Treaty (1967), Nuclear Non-Proliferation Treaty (1968)
9 The spring of 1968, when Alexander Dubcek tried to reform communism in Czechoslovakia
10 He first warned Dubcek to reverse the reforms, then sent Warsaw Pact troops to re-establish Soviet control

Chapter 3

1 1975
2 The invasion of Afghanistan by the Soviet Union
3 The Soviet Union led a boycott of the 1984 Los Angeles Olympics
4 Poland
5 Strategic Defense Initiative – a plan to place satellites in orbit that could shoot down nuclear missiles fired at the USA
6 The USSR was ruled by a series of elderly leaders who suffered from ill-health. Three leaders died in office between 1982 and 1985
7 The USA and Soviet Union would abolish all land-based missiles with a range of 500–5,500 km
8 The Berlin Wall came down
9 Hard-line communists tried to remove him from power
10 25 December 1991

Index

Key terms are capitalised initially, in bold type with an asterisk.
Entry headings for topic booklets are shown in italics.

Acknowledgements
With thanks to Paulette Catherwood for additional authoring support

Picture Credits
The publisher would like to thank the following for their kind permission to reproduce their photographs:

(Key: b-bottom; c-centre; l-left; r-right; t-top)

Alamy Stock Photo: CTK 17, CSU Archives/Everett Collection Historical 4 & 26, David Cole 10bl, MARKA/eps 13, Keystone Pictures USA 47; **Getty Images:** Dirck Halstead/The LIFE Images Collection 7t & 70, Hulton-Deutsch Collection/Corbis Historical 7b, Keystone/Hulton Archive 8 & 30, Hulton Archive/Archive Photos 10c & 34, Universal History Archive/Universal Images Group 10br & 83, Edward Miller/Keystone/Hulton Archive 21, Bettmann 31, 40, 43, 46, 50 t & b, 52 & 66, Lehnartz/Ullstein bild 45, Keystone-France/Gamma-Keystone 59, DIANE-LU HOVASSE/AFP 85; **Mirrorpix:** Philip Zec 15; **The Herb Block Foundation:** A 1962 Herblock Cartoon 56; **NASA:** 71; **AKG Images:** Ullstein bild 75; **Bridgeman Images:** Ronald Reagan. President Reagan Addressing the Nation on the National Security Defense Initiative. ("Star Wars" Speech). The White House, Washington, D.C. March 23, 1983 (78); **The Mary Evans Picture Library:** 66 & 84.

Cover image: *Front:* **Getty Images:** adoc-photos/Corbis

All other images © Pearson Education

We are grateful to the following for permission to reproduce copyright material:

Text Credits
10 Princeton University Library: From the 'Long Telegram' sent from Moscow to Washington by the US ambassador to the Soviet Union, George Kennan, on 22 February 1946, Princeton University Library; **16 Curtis Brown Group Limited:** From a speech given by Winston Churchill on 5 March 1946 at Westminster College, Curtis Brown Group Limited; **16 Woodrow Wilson International Center for Scholars:** Nikolai Novikov, From the 'Novikov Telegram' sent from Washington to Moscow, Soviet Ambassador to the USA, on 27 September 1946, Woodrow Wilson International Center for Scholars; **21 Harry S. Truman:** Harry S. Truman, From "The Truman Doctrine speech delivered on 12 March 1947 to the US Congress"; **22 George**

C. Marshall: George C. Marshall, From a speech made by US Secretary of State, on 5 June 1947; 23 Andrey Vyshinsky: Andrey Vyshinsky, From a speech by the Soviet foreign minister, given at the United Nations in September 1947; **27 The North Atlantic Treaty:** "The Northern Atlantic Treaty", Washington D.C. – 4 April 1949 https://www.nato.int/cps/en/natolive/official_texts_17120.htm **33 Imre Nagy:** Imre Nagy, "Last-minute plea for support as Soviet tanks rolled into Budapest", on 4 November 1956; **33 Nikita Khrushchev:** M. Burlatsky, "Khrushchev and the first Russian spring: the era of Khrushchev through the eyes of his advisor", Charles Scribner's Sons, 30 April 1992, 978-0684194196; **42 United States of America Department of State:** "Address given by Nikita Khrushchev on the GDR and Berlin", Moscow, 10 November 1958, https://www.cvce.eu/content/publication/2003/3/11/c4ac0cf0-2432-4440-8a95da856e4f25a4/publishable_en.pdf **44 John F Kennedy:** Kennedy, "President speaking to the American people after his return from the Vienna Summit meeting in 1961.", http://www.presidentialrhetoric.com/historicspeeches/kennedy/berlincrisis.html **47 John F Kennedy:** From a speech given by Kennedy in a public square in Berlin on 26 June 1963, http://www.jfklibrary.org/Asset-Viewer/oEX2uqSQGEGIdTYgd_JL_Q.aspx **47 John F Kennedy:** John F. Kennedy giving the 'Ich bin ein Berliner' speech, on 26 June 1963, http://www.jfklibrary.org/Asset-Viewer/oEX2uqSQGEGIdTYgd_JL_Q.aspx **53 United States of America Department of State:** Dean Acheson, "A statement made by Dean Acheson, one of Kennedy's advisers", at a meeting held on 17October 1962, https://rgshistory.wordpress.com/the-cuban-missile-crisis-1962-2/ **55 Thomson Learning Inc:** Sergei Khrushchev, "Memoirs of Nikita Khrushchev. Volume 2: Reformer, 1945–1964", Thomson Learning Inc; **60 Cambridge University Press:** Pravda Article Justifying Intervention in Czechoslovakia. (1968). International Legal Materials, 7(6), 1323-1325 © American Society of International Law 1969, published by Cambridge University Press; **79 Simon and Schuster:** Ronald Reagan, "An American Life", Simon and Schuster, 1990; **84 Independent:** Robert Vielhaber, "Fall of the Berlin wall – 25 years on: 'we were always aware that another part of Berlin existed' ", on 31 October 2014, The Independent.